NEWTON
AT THE
MINT

PORTRAIT MEDAL OF NEWTON.

By Johann Croker, Chief Engraver of the Mint.

NEWTON
AT THE
MINT

BY

SIR JOHN CRAIG

C.B., LL.D.

CAMBRIDGE
AT THE UNIVERSITY PRESS
1946

Printed in Great Britain at the University Press, Cambridge
(Brooke Crutchley, University Printer)
and published by the Cambridge University Press
Cambridge, and Bentley House, London
Agents for U.S.A., Canada, and India: Macmillan

PREFACE

The biographies of Newton evade the work which provided his income during thirty years. General and even particular statements upon it both there and in less specialised histories are uncommonly wrong. It seemed worth while to put together a few facts about an interesting man and an interesting period.

Newton's monetary theories were examined in an article by Professor Shirras and myself in the *Economic Journal* for June 1945, but without access to his recommendations for the Great Recoinage, then hidden beneath the tide of war. On this point also the previously accepted account must be reversed.

J. H. C.

1946

CONTENTS

LIST OF PLATES

CONTRACTIONS

Sotheby = Catalogue of the Newton Papers, published by Messrs Sotheby for the sale in 1936 of the Portsmouth collection of papers left by Newton to his estate.

Newton MSS. = Those of the above sorted by Conduitt to the head 'Papers relating to the Mint by Sir I. Newton', with a few others, now in the Royal Mint. These include: Warden's Accounts; Master's Accounts.

Hist. MSS. Commission = Appendix to the *Eighth Report of the Royal Commission on Historical Manuscripts*, 1881.

Try.pp. = Calendar of Treasury Papers, that is, of letters received by the Treasury from other departments, preserved in the Public Record Office.

Shaw, Writers = Mint letters in the Public Record Office, edited by William A. Shaw, *Select Tracts and Documents illustrative of English Monetary History*, 1626–1730; 1896.

M.R. = Royal Mint Record Books.

Goldsmiths' Library, Vol. 62 = Volume of manuscripts, entitled Recoinage of 1696, in the Goldsmiths' Library, University of London.

Luttrell = Narcissus Luttrell, *A brief Historical relation of State Affairs from September* 1678 *to April* 1714; 1857.

Conduitt = John Conduitt, *Observations upon the present state of our Gold and Silver Coins*, 1730; first edition 1774.

Brewster = Sir David Brewster, *Memoirs of the Life, Writings and Discoveries of Sir Isaac Newton*, second edition 1860.

More = Louis Trenchard More, *Isaac Newton*, 1934.

de Villamil = Lt.-Col. R. de Villamil, *Newton the Man*, 1922.

CHAPTER I

NEWTON IN THE MINT

THE MINT IN 1696

THE MINT lay between the inner and outer walls of the Tower of London. It began between Byward and Bell Towers with the Master Worker's Lodgings on both sides of the road; thence an irregular line of workshops, stores, stables, coach-houses, and a score of residences, curved away along the foot of each wall, to end up at the Salt Tower with the 'Irish Mint', an extension built by Elizabeth for coinage of that country. These buildings were largely of wood; the chief of them were two storied; most were crazy with age, held up by timber shores and pinned together with clamps of iron. There were even gardens: one by the Jewel Tower for the Warden; another by the Constable's, for the Comptroller. The Mint was guaranteed entire independence of the Tower, but under Charles II's militaristic policy the growing garrison had invaded its privacy, occupied the 'Irish Mint', seized the Porter's house, the Smith's house and some clerks' dwellings, and had built barracks on a vacant site. A paved road between the two rows was lit at night by four oil lamps and policed by solitary sentries, themselves liable to break in and steal.[1]

Seigniorage on gold and silver coinage having been abolished, the Mint since 1666 had been supplied with funds by a customs duty on imported liquor. The Master accounted each year to auditors for expenditure but, con-

1 Plan of 26 February 1701, reproduced in *Mint Annual Report* for 1890, p. 28; Bell, *Chapel in Tower*, p. 187; Newton MSS. III, 416.

trary to present practice, the balance remaining, which in time amounted to several years' income, was carried forward indefinitely, in coin or bank notes in the Board's safe. Once only, in 1715, a part of the holding was invested in Exchequer bonds, to help the Treasury over a sticky patch. The produce of the drink tax could by law only be used for coinage of silver or gold, though this limitation was not regarded as applying to a balance in hand at a Master's death. Other services had to be met from other sources. Thus, the Great Seal and the many other seals, home and overseas, were paid for by the Privy Purse; even the renewal of copper coinage had to be financed from the Purse. The expenses of management of the tin trade were paid by the monarch's trustees for that monopoly. The Great Recoinage of silver, enormously costly and involving payments above the Mint price for old coin and purchase of silver plate, produced a new tax on windows, of which the effect is still visible in the blinded walls of old buildings.

The spending of the Mint's regular income was strictly controlled. Treasury sanction was needed for any new post, except of workmen, or increase of salary, or any building work beyond maintenance; and besides, a maximum of £3,000—after 1705, £3,500—in any one year was imposed by the law of 1666 on salaries, building, and 'other necessaries for assaying, melting down and coining'. The expenditure of the Mint outside this limit was mainly on the allowance for costs made to the Master for each pound weight of coin issued. The total expenditure from the coinage duties of the London Mint during Newton's Mastership averaged just over £7,500 a year.

The personnel of the Mint was disposed very differently from the hierarchy of a modern department. The Warden had been the supreme officer, the King's representative, the manager of its finances, the supervisor of the Master, and the judge or magistrate for all disputes in or touching the Mint. At the abolition of seigniorage, now a generation back, his individual functions had been reduced to overseeing the detection and prosecution of counterfeiters and clippers of coin, and acting as the traditional but routine channel for certain payments. But he also remained in theory the representative and champion of the Mint and its disciplinarian.

The Master Worker had of old been the contractor for coinage. He was now responsible for all Mint expenditure and was its chief executive officer, but still conducted the coinage under a contract with the Crown, which allowed him 6s. 6d. for every pound troy of gold coin issued and 1s. 4½d. for every pound of silver coin; of these receipts he gave no account. He subcontracted the actual work; the first stage, the melting and casting into coinage bars of the raw material, to anyone he chose at whatever price he could obtain; the conversion of those bars into coin he was bound to place with the Company of Moneyers at a price which was fixed by long usage. The Company was the descendant of the old guild of coiners, which had shrunk to a few master men on the introduction of machinery. They were governed by by-laws of their own making and an elected Provost, through whom they dealt with the rest of the Mint; recruited their numbers as they pleased by taking into apprenticeship sons and relatives; like the Melter, they hired such labour as they needed and bought their own tools, replacements and material, for the Mint provided only initial capital equipment.

The Comptroller started as a second check on the Master, for the benefit of those who brought bullion to be coined; he still kept and rendered the separate bullion account; in addition he was responsible for all building, and provision of all supplies and incidental services; and he tended to become the Mint's general business man. Most of his expenditure was under running contracts with tradesmen selected every few years.

These three opponents were combined in a Board. Bullion could only be received, or coin issued, in the presence of two of them or their deputies; for which purpose the Board met on Wednesdays. On Saturdays they sat for general business, submitted by one of the members.

Each of the other Mint officers enjoyed, or at times abused, appreciable autonomy. The fitness of the Melter's bars for coinage, and of coin for issue, was decided by the King's Assayer, whose independence was naturally absolute. He also ran a large private practice in assaying for the market. The fineness of bullion on acceptance by the Mint was earlier, and later, checked by a Master's Assayer, but Masters had come to rely on the findings of the King's Assayer and to use the spare salary for other needs. The engravers had been selected and appointed by Charles II personally, and passed their duties on to their sons without further formality. The Superintendent of Meltings over-looked the Melter's work on behalf of the public, not of the Master. The Warden's clerks were sworn to obey, not the Warden, but the Lord High Treasurer. Even the Porter, holding his post from a higher authority and for life, bore himself as a potentate.

The work of the Mint was gold and silver coinage; any-thing else, medals, seals, even copper coinage, was held to be an extra, separately arranged with the individual officers concerned. Work was very spasmodic, and idle days or months could be spent in other occupations; some Moneyers, for instance, were farmers outside the town.

The gold coins struck were the 20s. piece, with, in smaller numbers, 10s., £2 and £5 pieces. Gold coin had

persistently risen above its nominal value; surpluses had
been pruned off by reductions of size from time to time;
but since the most recent of these, that of 1663, the 20s.
piece, initiated by the sovereign of Henry VII, and now
popularly dubbed a guinea, had usually changed hands at
about 21s. 6d. The other current gold coins, as well as the
antique weightier pieces and foreign gold, circulated at
proportionate values.

But in all men's minds the only true money of the
country was the silver coin—crowns, half-crowns, shillings
and sixpences; they were fashioned from time immemorial
of 925 parts of silver to 75 of copper; three and a half
centuries before, they had been of such size that 20s.
weighed a Saxon pound (about 11¼ oz. troy), but the
weight had been cut down again and again so that since
the reduction in the last years of Elizabeth there had been
no more than 62s. to the troy pound. The reduction to the
present weight of 66s. to the pound was made in 1816; the
drop to the present fineness of 500 parts of silver in 1,000
in 1920.

The typical proportion between these denominations
was 40 per cent in half-crowns and another 40 per cent in
shillings, 10 per cent in crowns and 10 per cent in sixpences,
as in the English recoinage of 1696–9 and the Scottish
recoinage of 1707–8. In normal years there was also included a trifle of 1½ per cent of the total in minor coin,
fourpences, threepences, twopences and pennies; but these
were too small and too few to be much use in ordinary
transactions. Change below the sixpence had to be found
in halfpence and farthings of base metal. In 1696 an
ephemeral issue of these coins in tin was being withdrawn
and replaced by copper. Some merchants had secured the
job on condition that they sent their copper blanks to the
Mint to be struck; conversely, when the Mint coined

copper under Charles II, it had bought copper blanks ready for striking.

The Mint had abandoned the old methods of coining by hand and hammer at the end of 1662, after trial runs which reached back to the days of Elizabeth. Gold was melted in small earthenware pots, silver in huge ones of iron that held a third of a ton, over charcoal fires. The liquid metal was ladled with long spoons into sand moulds, to be cast into little bars, hardly thicker than the intended coin. The bars, being passed to the Moneyers, were squeezed down to coin thinness by being passed three times between revolving iron cylinders of iron or steel. Modern practice, casting thicker bars, needs fifteen or more such passages. Each set of rolls was worked by four horses tramping round a cellar beneath. All further processes depended entirely on man power. Disks of proper size were first punched out of the strips which came from the rolling mills by machines rather like a letter copying press. As the cutting punch struck at an angle, the disks were bent; they were flattened again in another machine. Then they were weighed; excess of metal was corrected by filing the face of the disk; light disks were sent back to be remelted. Annealing followed, to soften the disks, which were then made more perfectly circular and impressed on the rims with a lettered inscription or with a graining—what we now call milling—by being rolled edgeways against engraved steel plates. This was the machine which all officers or others concerned had to swear to keep secret.

The coinage presses, though much larger, resembled the cutting presses. Two horizontal arms, each loaded with a hundredweight of lead at its tip, projected at waist height from the top. As a Moneyer inserted a blank between the two dies through an aperture in the foot of the press, four labourers pulled the arms violently; the capstan spun,

The ART of COINING.

Engrav'd for the Universal. Magazine 1750 for J. Hinton at the Kings Arms in St Pauls church yard London.

COINING PRESS: EDGE-MARKING MACHINE.

Universal Magazine 1750.

carrying with it the centre pillar to which it was attached and, as this in turn was fitted into a spiral in the housings, it crashed down and drove the die in its base against the blank and the latter against the nether die. These great machines could strike nearly a coin every two seconds— according to Newton;[1] the Moneyers put the average stroke at three a minute[2]—but the strain was so great that the labourers could only keep up work for fifteen minutes at a time. And few Moneyers were nimble enough to save their fingers indefinitely.

All this apparatus had been installed in the Mint at the end of 1662. It was costly, but was expected to bestow on the country the most perfect of coinages. The event, as events do, cheated the prophets. For the silver circulation was divided into two species by the new fashion. On the one hand, the machine-made article was uniform, deeply struck, compact, for it had been necessary to increase its thickness and therefore to reduce its diameter. Above all, its ornamented and perpendicular rim defeated the clipper. But the previous hand-struck coins were poor in comparison, with ill-defined periphery, thin, broad and soft, and a little worn and rubbed with age. Except for a handful struck after the Restoration, none was more recent than the Civil War, and quite a large proportion had been issued by Elizabeth, and some even by Edward VI. Consequently, the new coins came to be kept for savings, or export, or melting down for bullion, while the old had to bear the wear and tear of daily use. As the old coin deteriorated further, the practice, always endemic, of snipping or filing a scrap of silver off any better preserved specimens and reducing them to the common level, flared up, about 1686, into a widespread trade in which respectable bankers joined, while the blurring of the money let in

1 Newton MSS. i, 10; ii, 332.　　　2 Ibid. ii, 399.

a flood of counterfeits and foreign imitations. On top of distrust came inflation, begotten on the new system of credit by an expensive war. When people not only lost confidence in their currency but began to link its weakness with the change over from James II to William and Mary, something had to be done.

While the question was discussed, the guinea rose to a wavering 30s., and raw silver to 75s. a pound; at that price, 77 grains were a shillingsworth of silver. A new shilling weighed 93 grains; but the shillings in use 50 grains, or not much above. There were two schools, as over the gold standard in the mid-nineteen-twenties. Men who put domestic conditions first wanted the metal in the money unit to be cut, while those concerned with finance or foreign trade held that this was dishonest, and that the crown piece must continue to look the Spanish dollar and French écu in the face.

The day for amateurs had not yet darkened; many men of eminence in different spheres were consulted. From Cambridge Newton replied that the face value of silver coin must be brought into line with the market price of bullion. Analysing alternatives by the light of nature, he recommended withdrawal of clipped coin, in stages settled by denominations and reigns, addition of 25 per cent to the face value of good silver left in circulation, and corresponding reduction by a fifth of the weights of silver coin issued for the future. The sole objection seemed to him the unfairness to tax revenues, landlords, creditors generally and persons with fixed incomes, of the consequent rise of commodity prices. But he looked for a rapid correction of the position of all but investors in Government stocks. In view of the damage to public credit in mulcting supporters of the war, 'A Parliament may perhaps think itself concerned in Honour to take some care' to prevent this injustice. Accordingly, with apologies for a restraint of trade, Newton proposed a Price Control Board for the period of the war, either to reduce prices to the level of last winter, or prevent their further rise, or at least limit their increase. This Board in his conception was to operate only on the Chartered Companies of London. The Companies' instructions to their members, and the dominance of the country's trade by London, would—in his opinion— secure a temporary success, individual abuses excepted. Save as a vote for reduction of the metal content of coin, this academic disquisition added no more to the discussion than the plea of Christopher Wren, the architect, for a new unit of account, and a decimal system of coinage.[1]

While orthodox thus far, Newton thought that a shrinkage of the total face value of the coin circulation, which he expected, would of itself raise commodity prices. He accepted as an axiom that all taxation fell ultimately on land; and therefore agreed that in principle new taxes, in which he included implicitly control of prices, ought not to be imposed on trade.

Lowndes of the Treasury, lately promoted to Secretary, held that on grounds of history and theory alike the coin value of silver must be reduced, but, for the sake of a small economy, proposed raising the face value of the coins instead of lowering their weight. A 93-grain coin was to be called 1s. 3d., which on paper came to the same thing as dropping a shilling to 75 grains, as others had suggested. Indeed, for this, the commonest denomination, Lowndes proposed to do both. But he was positive that the bad coins must be withdrawn at once.[2] John Locke, the philosopher of the

---

1 Manuscripts entitled Recoinage of 1696; Vol. 62 in Goldsmiths' Library.
2 William Lowndes, *A Report containing an Essay for the Amendment of the Silver Coins*, 1695.

Whigs, retorted that values were and would continue to be, measured solely in silver, the metal, coined or uncoined, and that all these proposals were idle and unjust. He recommended that the worn coins should remain in circulation, but be reduced in the hands of their holders to values commensurate with their worn state, that is by about half. Guineas, being in his view but convenient merchandise, should be let float to what price they would. To complete his theory, copper coin should be avoided, and paper money was anathema.[1] Cutting across the ideas of both, the Chancellor of the Exchequer, Charles Montagu, drove Parliament to enact the compulsory recoinage of all handstruck silver coin, without any change of standards. The whole cost was borne by the Treasury, provided the coin was handed in by the due dates; those who brought their light coin late lost what it had dropped in weight. Montagu also forced through other measures which put a ceiling of 22s. on the guinea's value.

The credit given to Newton for these measures is doubly wrong. The Great Recoinage was a social crime, and its principles had not been advocated by him. In its early course it was attended by riots and commercial crises, and it compelled the Bank of England to stop cash payments. Its total cost to the Treasury and to remote or ignorant owners of coin must have been some five millions sterling[2] —more than a year's revenue of the Government. The effect of these sacrifices was to fit the silver circulation for export, and to set a relation between bullion and coin which cut off all normal flow of silver to the Mint; Conduitt in

1 Goldsmiths' Library, Vol. 62; John Locke, *Further Observations concerning raising the value of Money...*, 1695.

2 Liverpool, *Treatise on the Coins of the Realm*, 1805, p. 75, gives estimates from £2,200,000 to nearly £3,000,000 for cost to Exchequer. Feavearyear, *Pound Sterling*, 1831, p. 131, put loss to individuals at £1,000,000 as a minimum. But it was probably more than double this.

1730 wrote that since December 1701 'no silver has been imported to the mint but what was forced thither',[1] the circulation of silver coin in England immediately before the recoinage was estimated by Newton at nearly £12,000,000;[2] a hundred years later, with Scotland also to cover and twice the population, the silver circulation had fallen to below £3,000,000; most of the damage was done soon after the recoinage, and halfway through the century the bulk of the coin was again unrecognisable.[3] Further, all the principles were settled before Newton came to the Mint; the laws passed, the proclamations published; some of the new coin issued, and more of the old collected. He was still a famous University Professor, who had printed little but the *Philosophiae Naturalis Principia Mathematica*, now eight years old.

1 Conduitt, p. 11.   2 Newton MSS. 11, 608, 625, 628.
3 Liverpool, op. cit. p. 2

CHAPTER II

WARDEN

I N 1691, well before Newton's black year, John Locke
had tried to get him the Comptrollership of the Mint,
which he would then have gladly accepted. In the late
autumn of 1695, there were rumours that he was to be
made Master Worker; next spring, that he was to become
Comptroller. Newton wrote to Edmund Halley, the
astronomer, on 14 March 1696 to contradict this gossip:
'I neither put in for any place in the Mint, nor would
meddle with Mr Hoare's post, were it offered to me.'[1]
Hoare had been Comptroller since 1663. Five days later,
on 19 March, Montagu, the Chancellor of the Exchequer,
who was also President of the Royal Society, wrote to this
most distinguished of its Fellows:

I am very glad that at last I can give you a good proof of
my friendship and the esteem the King has of your merits.
Mr Overton, the Warden of the Mint, is made one of the
Commissioners of the Customs and the King has promised me
to make Mr Newton Warden of the Mint, the office is the most
proper for you 'tis the Chief Officer in the Mint, 'tis worth five
or six hundred pounds p.An., and has not too much bus'ness
to require more attendance than you may spare....[2]

The attractions were overstated, for the Warden's salary
was only £400. The offer needs no more recondite explanation than Montagu's own that he would not suffer
the lamp which gave so much light to lack oil. The
appointment was always filled from outside the Mint. The
white-haired, chubby man with the long nose and broad

1 More, pp. 435, 436.   2 Sotheby, 148.

jaw accepted at once; his appointment under the Privy Seal is dated 13 April;[1] he took the oath to keep secret the edging apparatus on 2 May.[2] He retained, in addition to his new office, the emoluments of his Cambridge Fellowship and his Lucasian Professorship of Mathematics.

Chief Officer the Warden had ceased to be; the new incumbent, studying the past of his post, recommended a return to that primacy, for he found the upper officers of the Mint disunited and self-seeking.[3] This, in all likelihood, was also the motive behind an appeal to the Treasury, within a month or two of taking office, for an increase of his salary, on the grounds that it was below the dignity of his post, that the Master had more than the Warden, that other salaries had been raised for the recoinage, and that the Warden's duties, too, had grown.[4] It was certainly a matter of principle, not of strain; Newton had money and leisure enough to make no use of the Warden's residence; he is said to have lived for a while hard by in Haydon Square, in the Minories,[5] and, if so, it can only have been at this time; in the autumn he settled down permanently in the house in Jermyn Street, where Jules' Hotel afterwards stood, a good half hour from the Mint. The Treasury parried the application with a promise of a later gratuity (16 June 1696).

The Mint was already in spate with the recoinage. The old coin was received by the Exchequer, cast in the Treasury gardens into small ingots, and carted to Tower Hill. The Mint had thrust the garrison back into the Tower, where the soldiers slept three a bed; turned the Comptroller's garden into a melting house; doubled some machines and trebled others; the Moneyers had by May

1 M.R. 5, 26.   2 Newton MSS. 1, 62.

3 Ibid. 1, 8.   4 Try.pp. xxxviii, 48.

5 Timbs, *Curiosities of London*, 1867, pp. 566, 567.

increased their horses to 33, and their men to 160;[1] later these rose to 500. Double shifts must have been worked, for working hours were extended to twenty a day for six days a week. The Warden, however, had nothing to do with organising and stimulating. That duty fell in theory on the Master Worker; in practice, on the Comptroller and on a special King's clerk, Thomas Hall, appointed in February with a salary equal to the Warden's to see the Master through. In July Newton had, like all the other officers, to appoint a deputy at each of the five temporary Mints in country towns. These appointments were personal, but Newton does not appear to have used his patronage specially for friends; at least, Edmund Halley owed to Hoare his assignment as Deputy Comptroller at Chester. It seems, however, to have been Newton, who had the civil servant's appreciation of uniformity, who drafted the common form of appointment used by his colleagues. About the same time, he drew up the stately document which, as Warden, he issued to all Mint staff, to protect them from the Press-gang.

These country Mints were pretty bad in some ways; the Deputy Master of Norwich had all his property confiscated and spent several years in gaol; the Deputy Comptroller at Exeter had still not cleared his accounts when he died in his next post of 'Ambassador to the Pirates of Madagascar'.

The Warden, as such, was concerned only with breaches of the peace. When he wrote to the Chester Deputy Comptroller (21 June 1697) about tightening up the examination of coin before issue, he did so explicitly on behalf of the latter's chief. The Deputy Master, Clarke, evaded these directions; he also issued coin out of their turn to persons who had brought silver to the Mint. The other two Deputies, Weddell and Halley, stymied him by

1 Try.pp. xxxviii, 19.

locking all coin in the safe.[1] Clarke turned on his colleagues. After an exchange of Billingsgate in the public office, Weddell spat in his face; Clarke challenged Weddell to a duel, but did not await his arrival on the challenge field; then he hastened to London to pull strings, while Halley called in Newton's influence to have the 'proud, insolent fellow' removed.[2] The Board's impartial rebuke, though signed also by Hoare, has the Newtonian stamp:

We are much concerned to hear of your continued quarrels ...we believe both sides much in the wrong and resolve to come and hear it ourselves....Till we come let there be no further quarrelling...for the Mint will not allow of the drawing of swords and assaulting of any, nor ought such language we hear has been, be used any more amongst you.[3]

Another Board ruling, in the next February, on manners seems also Newton's. The clerks at Chester were bidden to cease affronting their superiors by wearing hats and swords in the Mint Office, as in London only upper staff were allowed to appear on the premises in full kit.[4] Simultaneously with the news of brawls at Chester, Newton had to cope with a larger ploy in London. It began on a night in late June 1697, when a tipsy officer of the garrison tried to break into a Mint residence and ran a sword through the coat tails of the householder. A sentinel refused assistance; a file of musketeers had to be summoned from inside the Tower. Lord Lucas, Lieutenant of the Tower, on some garbled tale, to safeguard his sentries from the Mint, gave orders that they should fire on the drunk and disorderly. 'A bloody discipline,' wrote Newton, '...why should the people who live in the Mint be so terrified as to leave their habitations in it?'

1 M.R. Chester, 42, 50, 52.　2 Brewster, II, 142; More, p. 340.
3 M.R. Chester, 52.　4 Ibid. 70.

Sentinels inside the Mint should, he said, be grouped in numbers sufficient to overpower resistance. He went across and interviewed Lucas on 1 July, but only irritated him into an aggressive mood. On the morrow, his Lordship, on the ground that the soldiers when they had exhausted their credit with the Army victuallers used any current pay to get supplies from the Moneyers' staff, stopped all entry of food or drink into the Mint. The workmen were with the greatest difficulty dissuaded from striking and their output fell by half. Next day, the 3rd, one of the melting-house men, Philip Atherton, was arrested with the Lieutenant's connivance on the Mint premises for beating up a head constable in the town to extricate his wife from custody. Atherton's apprehension was a clear breach of the ancient, though possibly outworn, privilege of Mint personnel of freedom from arrest or trial except by the Warden. The same afternoon, a Tower warder, who had taken some visitors round the coining rooms, as was common, was stopped at the exit by the Gate Porter, who demanded a tip, and refused coppers as unbecoming in the Mint. The warder slipped the visitors away by another door, and returned to deal with the Porter, 'whence arose such a tumultuous concourse of people as rendered unsafe the money which was then coming down the street of the Mint in trays'. Personal negotiation having failed, Newton complained to the Treasury; to which 'scandalous' letter, as he called it, Lord Lucas replied with denials, and complaints of the turbulence of the Mint. The warder, for instance, had been beaten by the Porter, his mother, his father and his son, and only went back to say mildly that if this had happened outside the Mint, he would have kicked the Porter. And on 24 July, three days before Newton's letter, a Mint labourer had galloped two of the Mint horses against a sentinel and driven him into a refuge, while the Warden's clerk, Fowles (to whom Newton was indebted for a lively account of the passivity of previous Wardens), exhorted the horseman to drag the soldier away by the ears and shoot him through the head. If the Lieutenant's lady, looking on the affray from an upper window had not called the guard, the sentinel might have been done to death.[1] The upshot seems to have been a prohibition on the sale of drink by the Mint to the garrison, and an eventual reduction of the passages between Mint and Tower to two.

But strife between the two bodies, mostly over disputed buildings, lasted to the end of Newton's life.

These private piques occurred in the middle of a struggle with more powerful folk. In 1696 the House of Commons struck at the Mint with a Committee of inquiry into its 'Miscarriages' or, as we would say, abuses. Newton was the official witness on its organisation and functions; his evidence[2] was adopted almost verbatim as the Committee's recital on those points. On others, other Mint witnesses were called; the Deputy Wardens, for example, were dragged up from the country; among the hostile witnesses was William Challoner. This versatile person first comes to light during the recoinage controversy in 1695 as author of a pamphlet[3] to advocate that the new coins should be made of the weight to which the old had been reduced. Next February, 1696, he approached the Privy Council[4] as well as Montagu[5] on the incompetence of the Mint and his own discoveries of better coining methods. With Parliament on the alert, he published these views, and was heard by the Committee on Mint Miscarriages. He told

1 Newton MSS. III, 409, 344.   2 Ibid. I, 2.
3 William Challoner, *Reasons humbly offered against passing an Act
   for raising £1,000,000 for making good the deficiency of the
   Clipt-Money.*
4 M.R. 3, 197.   5 Try.pp. LXVI, 53.

them in particular that the Mint made counterfeit coin, and allied itself with counterfeiters; in general, that it was staffed by specialists, of whom each knew but his one job, and needed the supervision of a man of all-round experience. As proof of his suitability, he submitted two inventions which would stop counterfeiting; a groove should be put in the rims of genuine coin, to prevent copying by casts and moulds, and the relief should be heightened till it could only be struck by the most powerful of presses. He could convert the Mint presses to the necessary horse-power at a small initial cost and with big continuing economies. The Committee bade Newton fetch apparatus for Challoner to demonstrate his claims (5 February 1697).[1] Newton refused, since the Mint machines were secret.[2] But, having experimented in the Mint, he informed the Committee that the projects were impracticable. Their Report found fault with the Mint on many another point, and recommended Challoner's inventions for adoption.[3]

Newton clapped the inventor into irons in Newgate, where he lay for seven weeks. Once free, the prisoner invoked the immunity of witnesses; claimed consideration for the ruin into which he had been plunged, and for the abortion in gaol, to the nation's loss, of a book to expose the Mint that he had conceived. At the Parliamentary inquiry which this provoked next Session (March 1698), Newton based Challoner's arrest on a suspicion that he intended another felony; the accounts show that £9. 10s. was spent on developing this suspicion.[4] The Warden went on with a biography of Challoner. Seven years before, he had been but a poor workman in the new trade of japanning; a career

---

1 Newton MSS. 1, 506.   2 Ibid. 1, 497.
3 Rev. Rogers Ruding, *Annals of the Coinage of Great Britain*, ed. 1840, ii, 465 ff.
4 Newton MSS. 1, 476.

of crime had raised him to the dignity of a residence in Kensington, a dinner service of plate and the clothes of a gentleman. Challoner had become the most accomplished counterfeiter in the kingdom of English or foreign coin; an inventor of better ways of casting and moulding; so nice an artist of dies that it galled him to spoil their perfection by use. As sidelines, he had stolen horses to furnish capital for a coiner's headquarters in the country; £200 had been obtained from the Bank of England for information about a forgery of their documents; the Exchequer had been robbed of £1,000 by an elaborate trick. This sum had been offered by the Government for betrayal of the source of propaganda which was being spread about London on behalf of James II. Challoner got hold of a copy of the objectionable circular, had forty more copies printed, informed on the printers and pocketed the cash. And, dog eating dog, he had also sent a fellow false coiner to the scaffold.[1]

The true intent of his appearance before the Committee on Miscarriages had been to coax out of them an appointment within the Mint, as a help to making flash coin outside it.

Challoner was overthrown—no mean achievement for a don pitted against a clever criminal, with hostile politicians as jury. He was convicted of false coining, drawn on a sledge to Tyburn and executed on 4 March 1699, and would have been hanged long before had he not turned King's evidence.[2] Newton ran the prosecution.

Transient troubles, these; to catch and convict clippers and false coiners was a permanent worry. Originally the duty of Sheriffs, this task had been drawn into the Mint just after the Restoration by a Warden's clerk. There being no police, he and his successors themselves seized and

1 Newton MSS. I, 492, 501.   2 Luttrell, IV, 489, 496.

took to court any wrongers of the coin of whom they could hear, but the sword of justice was also wielded, unreliably, by free-lance agents and informers, in hope of a reward or of a profit hidden in their bills of costs. The clerk's salary was paid from Mint funds proper; for all other expenses there was only the proceeds of offenders' confiscated properties. To complicate things, such goods were often forcibly claimed by other interests.

Newton's predecessors had left this work entirely to their clerks. The new Warden superintended it in detail; personally interviewed the accused and their solicitors; strove, and after becoming Master successfully, to better its organisation and finance. His day to day work comprised, for example, £5 'paid to Humphrey Hall to buy him a suit of clothes to qualify him for conversing with a gang of Coiners of note'.[1]

It was presumably to strengthen his hands in dealing with these criminals that Newton spent £14. 10s. of his own money on being made a Justice of the Peace for each of the seven Home Counties.[2] He also started the compilation of something like a case book to guide him on local practice. The rules of evidence, for instance, are thus illustrated. A house was searched on suspicion that the owner was a highwayman; instead, indications of clipping were found; the Mint prosecuted the man; the Judge sent them away to frame a sterner indictment, which they only got through the Grand Jury with difficulty. The prisoner, brought again before the Judge, pleaded that the articles were none of his, and that a charge of coin felony needed the evidence of two eyewitnesses; at which his Lordship burst out: 'The shears supply the place of one witness, the filings of another, and the rough clipped money of another.'[3]

1 Newton MSS. 1, 467. 2 Ibid. 1, 18 (misdated).
3 Ibid. 1, 482.

To secure finance, Newton, in his first six months, revived dormant Mint claims to confiscated goods against the Sheriffs of London and against the Chapter of Westminster; and won his case from a reluctant Treasury, which had to placate the Sheriffs from other funds. It was a barren victory. The recoinage had stopped clipping. The rich clippers turned honest, the humbler became false coiners in swarms, but their poor goods were scarcely worth seizure. Most of the Warden's expenditure in subduing them, which indeed only amounted to £200 a year, had to be met by special Treasury grants.[1] Newton's activities, however, cleared the offenders out of London into places where they were hard for him to come at.

The work disgusted him, and he asked the Treasury to be relieved of it: 'I am exposed to the calumnies of as many coiners and Newgate Solicitors as I examine or admit to talk with me.....'Tis the business of an Attorney and belongs properly to the King's Attorney and Solicitor General....I humbly pray that it may not be imposed on me any longer.'[2]

There was no pity for the wretched transgressors. The Mint, indeed, finding that the severity of the law made magistrates unwilling to convict, proposed the abolition of the death penalty for the less heinous offences; just as it got Sheriffs quit of liability to reward successful informers, because Sheriffs managed to prevent success. It was a question of efficiency, not of kindness. Newton, who continued to be consulted in later life on this bit of Warden's business, was always against pardons or remissions on the grounds that these disheartened the Mint agents and that criminals returned to their vomit.

In 1697 Newton compiled an administrative synopsis of the several coinage operations, speed of melting, speed

1 Try.pp. xxxix, 38, 57.   2 Newton MSS. i, 438.

of the different types of machine, number of hands required on each, and of the technique of assaying gold and silver.[1] Being a man of his hands, he made himself a finished master of the last process, which he practised from time to time on old or alien coin. His assayer's furnace and a touchstone attributed to him are still preserved in the Mint. But he gave assaying no high rank, intellectual or social; he defined it as a 'manual trade', for which restless or inventive minds would be unsuitable,[2] and demurred at a candidate for employment conducting himself to the Officers of the Mint 'in such a manner as is not to be borne in an Assaymaster'.[3] He cared not a whit for scientific advances towards obtaining complete purity of metals or measuring their fineness in absolute terms, as we shall see from his criticisms of the Gold Trial Plate of 1707.

Newton applied his empiric skill in 1697 to the assay of Scots coin current in England. James I had enacted that it should exchange for English at the rate of twelve Scots pounds, shillings or pence for one English, and that henceforward the twelvefold Scots piece should be made identical with its southern counterpart. The first edict had generally endured; the second had been altered by later ordinances. The Tower Mint's knowledge of Scots law and practice at the Edinburgh Mint, for which the Warden made the peculiar Scots weights, was minute on some points, and as remarkable for ignorance of others. Newton worked out from this information the lower weight of Scots coin; it agreed with what he found on weighing samples. But the slightly lower fineness of such coin, which he detected by assay, he ascribed to careless work, though it also was exactly as prescribed by recent Scots law. On these

---

1 Newton MSS. 1, 10, 11.　　　　2 Ibid. 1, 98.
3 Ibid. 1, 97.

findings, after deducting something for the greater vari-
ability of Scots coin and its liability to be counterfeited, he
valued 10s. Scots on its bullion content, not at 10d., but at
9d., and he won the Treasury to instruct collectors of taxes
only to accept it at the lesser figure.[1] Whereat the coin
ceased to pass in England. A peculiar feature of this
achievement is that on 23 January 1697, the Scots Government had already made approximately this change so far
as English milled coin was concerned;[2] clearly, the new
valuation was unknown at the Tower.

Only a few days after the Scots had thus beaten him to
the post, Newton received, on 26 January 1697, Bernoulli's
challenge to the world to solve the mathematical problem
dubbed the brachistochrone. He sat down to it at four in
the afternoon after his return from the Mint, and solved
it by four in the small hours.[3] Occasionally, from 1695 to
1697, he was engaged in revising the educational syllabus
of Christchurch, advising on purchase of books or examining scholars. His professional duties at Cambridge
remained in abeyance; his elucidation of the moon's
orbit from Flamsteed's observations which had begun in
1694, continued to be worked upon till December 1698,
though in April 1695 Newton intended to drop it,
and the astronomer understood that by January 1696
the new theory and its general results were pretty well
established.[4]

By June 1698 the country Mints had finished work,
except for a little clearing up, and were officially closed,

1 Newton MSS. III, 2.
2 Edward Burns, *Coinage of Scotland*, 1887, II, 517. The date 1697
for Newton's proposals is given in the text of his draft (Newton MSS.
III, 2) and other details therein show that it was not early in the year;
twenty years later, by a slip of memory, Newton ascribed his valuation
to 1702 (Try.pp. CCVIII, 43).

3 More, p. 474.   4 Ibid. pp. 406, 423, 434, 477.

and their staffs disbanded for the most part. The Tower
Mint also had dropped to normal; indeed, the extra allow-
ances for increased work had ceased in August 1697;[1] the
coinage of 1698 was small; that of 1699 still smaller, and in
June 1699 the additional machinery installed for the
recoinage both there and in the country was sold to the
Moneyers.[2]

Not the facts of Mint business but diplomacy must have
settled the phraseology of Newton's letter to Flamsteed in
which, on 6 January 1699, he refused to have a reference
to his inquiries into the moon's orbit published: 'I do not
love to be printed on every occasion...or to be thought by
our own people to be trifling my time about them [sc.
mathematical problems] when I should be about the King's
business.'[3] The puzzle was solved; its interest exhausted.
So far was he from abandoning scientific pursuits that in
the same year or the next he wrote many thousand words
on the advantages of the Julian over the Gregorian Calendar
to which Great Britain clung till 1752, and on a more
symmetrical variant of his own which divided the years at
the equinoxes and solstices into six winter months of
30 days, five summer months of 31 days and one summer
month of 30 days which became 31 in leap year. But with
his usual practical sense, he added that he did not think
that the number of days in a month should be altered
'without the consent of a good part of Europe'; that the
choice lay between the two Calendars in actual use; and
that he recommended, without pressing it, adoption of the
current continental date without their Calendar[4]—thus

---

1 Newton MSS. 1, 104.   2 M.R. 6, 64.
3 Brewster, 11, 149; More, p. 462.
4 Brewster, 11, 246; More, p. 488; Sotheby, 222. The Gregorian
Calendar which had been used by the principal Roman Catholic States
from 1582 to 1587 was adopted by Protestant German States, Netherlands and Denmark in 1700.

leaving the further question of principle open for the next hundred years. In August 1699 he exhibited to the Royal Society the sextant which he had invented and made himself; it was suffered to drop from sight and memory and was reinvented long after and brought into use as Hadley's sextant.[1]

1 More, p. 487.

CHAPTER III

THE MASTER'S NEW BROOM

THOMAS NEALE died on or shortly before 20 December 1699,[1] and Newton was appointed, on Boxing Day, the 26th, to the more lucrative post of Master and became responsible for Mint administration. This translation was unusual. The last choice of an existing Mint officer for the Mastership had been that of Sir Richard Martin, likewise from the post of Warden, in the reign of Elizabeth; after Newton, no Master was ever appointed from within the Mint. A proper reason would have been that Newton had shown himself the most energetic and conscientious of the last half dozen Wardens, while of the last two selections for Master, Slingsby got into such a financial mess that he was summarily ejected by the arm of the law; whilst Neale had ceded his duties as well as his income to creditors, and was only saved from bankruptcy by the Great Recoinage.

But Newton's preferment was probably due to the enormous esteem in which he was held. On his death, twenty-seven years later, the Mastership was offered to the Reverend Samuel Clarke, whose only qualification or claim was his exposition of Newton's mathematics and physics. When Clarke refused the job as not fitting his cloth, it was given to John Conduitt, an otherwise undistinguished M.P., who had married Newton's stepniece and had since been closely associated with him, and who devoted £1,000 to a solatium for Clarke.[2]

A more romantic explanation of the second or both of

---

1 Luttrell, IV, 597.   2 More, p. 454.

Newton's appointments was given by a woman writer of piquant paragraphs, Mrs Manley, in 1710, and by Voltaire long after in his *Lettres Philosophes*. They averred that Newton was made Master by the Lord Treasurer, Lord Halifax, then Charles Montagu, for the sake of his attractive stepniece, Catherine Barton. Mrs Manley says that Halifax got Miss Barton's 'worthy ancient parent a good post for connivance';[1] Voltaire, that Newton became 'grand maître des monnaies' by reason of his niece's charm. Now, in March 1696, when the Warden's post was proferred, Catherine was a girl of fifteen, living in the country, whom there is no reason to think that Montagu, not yet a widower, had even seen, but in December 1699, when Newton was made Master, Montagu had already fallen from place and power.

Moreover, Catherine did not join up with Montagu till much later; in 1700, she was living with her uncle. On 5 August 1700, Newton wrote to her at Mr Gyre's house at Pudlicot, near Woodstock, Oxfordshire:[2]

I had your two letters and am glad the air agrees with you and though the fever is loth to leave you yet I hope it abates, and that the remains of the small pox are dropping off apace. Sir Joseph Tilley is leaving Mr Tell's house and it is probable I may succeed him. I intend to send you some wine by the next carrier which I beg the favour of Mr Gyre and his Lady to accept of. My Lady Norris thinks you forget your promise of writing to her, and wants a letter from you. Pray let me know by your next how your face is and if your fever be going. Perhaps warm milk from the cow may abate it.

I am your very loving uncle, Is. NEWTON.

The tone of the letter implies that niece and uncle had been in close contact before she went into the country to recover

1 More, p. 468. 2 Newton MSS. II, 29.

from smallpox. It is certain that she brought the letter back to the house in Jermyn Street, for Newton used the back of it to draft his report of 7 July 1702 to the Treasury.

From 1701 to 1703 Montagu was suffering actual impeachment and like trials. It was 1706 before he was clear of his troubles. On 10 April he was appointed a Commissioner for negotiating the Union with Scotland; on the 12th he made handsome testamentary provision for Catherine on his death. He also bought her an annuity of £200 a year, apparently on 26 October 1706, which was temporarily vested in Newton. Newton himself drafted some notes for the will, and the document for the final transfer of the annuity to Catherine.[1] So it was presumably in April 1706 that Catherine went to superintend Montagu's household. In 1710 and 1711, however, he maintained her in a separate establishment.

The lady seems to have had a clear head. Gossip about 1711 was that she pressed Montagu hard for more money.[2] On 1 February 1713 he duly made a new will in which he left her £5,000, the Rangership and house in Bushey Park, which he had acquired in 1709 with other rentals to pay for its upkeep. Newton again drafted parts of the settlement.[1]

Montagu died on 19 May 1715. Sometime in the next two years Catherine sent her uncle a pathetic little note:[3] 'I desire to know whether you would have me wait here... or come home.' Home was now in St Martin's Street, off Leicester Square, whither Newton had moved in 1710 after a year in Chelsea. She came home all right, for the blank page has been used by both uncle and niece; these endorsements only show that it must have been originally written before August 1717; and that she had then 'come home'.

1 Sotheby, 196.   2 Mrs Manley, *New Atlantis*.
3 Sotheby, 176.

On 26 August she married John Conduitt. The married couple long stayed on with Newton, but probably did not accompany him to Pitt's Buildings, Church Street, Kensington, when Newton, in failing health and for the sake of the country air, repaired there in January 1725, though he kept on the St Martin's Street house. At any rate, Conduitt had taken a house of his own before Newton's death, and wrote of Newton's 'coming' to London, as if his own residence were there. It is pretty clear that in his last illness the old man had less constant attention than for six or seven years before.

To bind together these scattered dates, there is a statement of Conduitt's that Catherine lived with her uncle before and after her marriage for nearly twenty years.[1] An approximate conclusion is that she joined Newton on, or soon after, his taking the house in Jermyn Street in the autumn of 1696, for she seems to have been on the spot when, on 26 January 1697, he disposed of Bernoulli's challenge problem in an evening.[2] She left him for Montagu in April 1706, as soon as financial arrangements had been completed, and did not return to her uncle for possibly two years after Montagu's death. Some period spent in the St Martin's Street house after the Master had gone to Kensington, and possibly the whole span, must reckon towards the 'nearly twenty years'.

There is no doubt that Catherine Barton was under the protection of Montagu for some nine years, living in and superintending his house at one time, but in 1711 in a separate establishment of her own. For Swift visited her there. It is certain also that Newton advised her on the business side of the affair. He was no more called upon to boycott a morganatic alliance without benefit of clergy than was Marlborough to criticise his sister's amours with

1 More, p. 457.   2 Ibid. p. 570.

James II. But it is equally clear that the liaison did not bear on Newton's own fortunes. A pendant to these happenings is a testimonial Newton made out for a servant in 1722:

> Mary Anderson lived with me two or three years and, so far as I know, behaved herself honestly, but upon a falling out between her and another servant, I parted with her.

So he wrote, but perceived an ambiguity and altered 'lived with me' to 'served me as a cook'.[1]

A Master of the Mint was hung about with parchments. Neale died in December 1699; Newton became Master on the morrow of his fifty-seventh birthday, that being the beginning of the Mint year. On 10 January, a Royal Warrant empowered him to act under Neale's Indenture 'as a new Indenture cannot suddenly be made'.[2] On 2 March the appointment was formally conferred by Royal Letters Patent under the Great Seal, which contained the express condition that he execute a new Indenture within two months.[3] During the year he swore at the Treasury to discharge the duties of Master faithfully and was given a certificate to that effect.[4] The Indenture, or contract between Master and Crown, a lengthy document which defined the rights, pay and procedure, of all sections of the Mint, was only executed on 23 December. A month later, on 21 January 1701, procedure concluded with the new Master's entering into a bond for £2,000, backed by two sureties, as insurance for the Exchequer in case of his delinquency. From its leisureliness, much of this procedure was evidently regarded in informed quarters as a ceremonious survival. It was repeated three times for Newton, at his first appointment, on the accession of Anne, and on that of George I, with increasing procrastination; but, in spite of frequent changes of Masters, only two Indentures sufficed from his death to the Battle of Waterloo.

Newton, on the other hand, studied the documents with the earnestness proper to a civil servant; he made stylistic amendments in the draft of the Indenture, and reinserted an obsolescent proviso about the Moneyers' remuneration. When machinery was adopted, the Corporation of Moneyers were granted, in addition to the fees payable by the Master, a penny from general Mint funds for each pound weight of silver coinage, provided the year's coinage comprised the due proportion of small coins, penny to fourpence. This condition was dropped during the Great Recoinage, during which the small coins were not struck. Newton now revived it. The small coins were too rare to be of any use in buying and selling—Newton called them 'curiosities and toys for children'—and only the penny was used during Newton's lifetime for the Maundy ceremonial. Their ratio to all silver strikings had been reduced years before to $1\frac{1}{2}$ per cent, but on their inclusion 11 per cent of the Moneyers' remuneration was made, on paper, to depend. In fact the proviso never thereafter affected the payments made to the Moneyers, though it is not likely that it was satisfied, for example, in 1711 when £71,512 out of a total coinage of £76,781 was derived from a special purchase of plate and was required to be coined only into shillings and sixpences. Three years after this Indenture, steps had to be taken to increase the Moneyers' remuneration.[1]

On the first renewal of his papers of appointment, in 1702, Newton argued, against his personal interest, that, on precedent, security should be exacted at an earlier stage, and so urged the Attorney General, with the support

1 Newton MSS. II, 516.

of extracts from documents back to the reign of Edward III. The shaken lawyer could only reply that it did not much matter and that the last precedent had best be followed.[1]

Newton indeed had little success when he delved into law. It was natural, when he was assessed in 1700 under the new Militia Act to provide two soldiers, to claim immunity for the Mint by reason of the old and wide exemption of Mint personnel from taxation.[2] This line failing, he opposed in 1721 an order to deduct income tax from Mint salaries on the ground that the taxing statute had not set aside the requirement of the Coinage Acts that Mint funds must be devoted solely to coinage.[3] In 1702 he had tried to help the Exchequer by the theory that though the coinage duties could not be used to provide coronation medals, they might be spent on buying and coining bullion, and the resulting coin expended on silver and labour for the medals. The Law Officers of the Crown in each case took the contrary view.

At different times he drafted bills or clauses for Mint and other legislation. Some perished because the Government did not accept their principle. Those that did pass to the statute book were redrawn with more simplicity and less completeness. Modern legislation prefers that Newtonian form. In all these points, Newton seems to have been technically, but the lawyer politicians practically, right. He had a nice sense of the meaning of words.

Two matters of substance were involved in this first appointment. The security required of the last Master had been £15,000. Newton demurred to so great a sum, which he attributed to the dubious financial history of Neale, who 'having spent a great estate and being in debt made his way into the place by granting half thereof to other officers

---

1 Newton MSS. 1, 73, 387, 395, 399, 407.
2 M.R. 7, 9; 7, 52.   3 Newton MSS. 1, 346, 359.

in the Mint';[1] and he produced extracts of the documents of all preceding Masters back to Richard III, to show that each had been asked for only £2,000. A reduction to that figure was conceded. Montagu, the late Lord Treasurer, offered to be one of the sureties,[2] but was not acceptable to the new régime. The sureties for Newton were on this and later occasions persons subordinate to him in the Mint, his Melter, the King's clerk or his Deputy Master.[3]

The Mastership since the middle of Elizabeth's reign had always been conferred for life; now, in accord with one recommendation of the Committee on Mint Miscarriages, it was granted only during the Crown's pleasure. A vain attempt was made to undo this innovation after Newton's death; he himself does not seem to have felt any concern over the less certain tenure. On the contrary, he parted at last with his University posts at the end of 1701, having given the pay of the Lucasian professorship to Whiston from the beginning of the year.[4]

Newton represented Cambridge in the House of Commons in 1689–90 and was defeated at the ensuing election. He was again elected for that University in February 1701 but, on the dissolution of Parliament in July 1702, refused to stand again: 'I have served you in this Parliament; other gentlemen may expect their turn in the next.'[5] In 1705 he came forward again as a candidate, but was defeated by an insurgence of country clergy. In spite of these incursions into politics, Newton's position was that of a civil servant; the distinction between that silent service and elective offices was not drawn till a little later. All questions of policy as well as of any unusual expenditure fell to the Treasury; the former, Newton not infrequently discussed

1 Newton MSS. 1, 64.   2 Ibid. 1, 66.
3 Ibid. 1, 65, 66, 67.   4 More, p. 488.
5 Sotheby, 162.

orally with the Lord Treasurer, or, when that office was put in commission, with the First Lord of the Treasury; with Lowndes and subordinates he does not seem to have had any contacts.

The strain was much lighter than falls on a modern head of a department. The volume of work was small; the system of contracts and subcontracts divorced the Master from most of the staff and their activities. It is quite likely that Newton never set foot in the coining rooms, and a visit to the melting house during experiments on casting copper appears to have been quite exceptional. For day to day oversight of the Master's office, he appointed a deputy, John Francis Fauquiere, a man of substance, a Director of the Bank of England, who had been Neale's financial agent. Fauquiere was given the salary of £60 a year allowed for the Master's Assayer; Newton, following recent practice, dispensed with this check on the King's Assaymaster.

Further, decisions on questions at large were vested in the Mint Board, on which the new Warden, Sir John Stanley, took formal precedence. Even on what was primarily the Master's business, Newton at times had to accept or circumvent the views of his colleagues. Thus, in 1709 he wrote to the Edinburgh Mint on petty points of formal accounting:

I have been slow to return an answer for fear that some of these things may be referred to Officers of the Mint with whom I sometimes find it difficult to agree and therefore what I now write you should be considered as coming not from an Officer of the Mint but from a personal friend.[1]

Moreover, large blocks of business, though brought before the Board, were considered to be primarily the affair of Warden or Comptroller. All legal or criminal work, for instance, went with the Wardenship. Newton was not even,

1 Newton MSS. III, 44.

so far as appears, concerned with a Bill which the Mint
promoted in 1701 to abolish the death penalty for passing
of counterfeit coin.[1] Nor did he deal personally with frauds
by two hierarchs of the Mint in that summer. Molyneux,
the Comptroller, reduced the apparent cost of repairing
his own residence, in order to get the project through the
Board and Treasury, by debiting, both in estimates and in
accounts, big items to the Warden's house; Mason, either
a joint or a deputy Comptroller, extorted cash for himself
and jewellery for his wife from contractors before he
would certify their bills.[2] Both were discharged.

Though the Board normally met twice a week, with a
third day at very busy times and long vacations at others,
attendance might be by deputy, and the records of the
Crown share of meals suggest from 1704 onwards that the
meetings or attendance fell very heavily indeed, except
in the years 1709-11.

Newton did all or most of his written work at home.

A bid by the Warden for increased power was defeated.
A little extra copper had to be added to each melt of gold
or silver to offset the differential effect of heat; the quantity
was not entirely stereotyped, but was modified to meet
changing experience. The Warden claimed the duty of
regulating it. Newton answered with thirty-four pages of
extracts from Elizabethan papers, and held him off.[3]

The new Master started with an administrative clean-up.
At the Restoration, Charles II had mulcted the lately errant
Mint of all its records. £55 was spent (1700 and 1701) on
replacing some of them with copies from diverse sources.[4]
The clerks were set to transcribe the tangled accounts and
correspondence of the recoinage. It can hardly be chance

1 M.R. 7, 37.   2 Try.pp. LXX, 9, 42; M.R. 7, 12, 13.
3 Hist. MSS. Commission 65(a) to 66(a).
4 Warden's Accounts.

that throughout the Newton régime copies and notes of letters and decisions were kept by the Mint much more fully than either before or after. A survey and ground plan of the premises were ordered to be made by one of the engraver's assistants, but the work had to be transferred, with a fee of £12. 18s., to an outsider, William Allingham, Gent.[1] His plan, dated 26 February 1701, is reproduced in the Mint Report for 1890. Abuses were limited by clear rules that Mint officers must pay for all but first decoration and for tenants' repairs of their residences, unless the damage was done by the Tower's artillery practice.[2] This last was heavy enough to warrant an official request from Newton: 'That the Gunner of the Tower do order the Guns in such a manner that upon firing they may do least harm to the glass windows of the Mint.'[3]

Other conscientious probing brought a conflict with the Moneyers. Charles II had formerly conferred the eventual charge of the new Mint machinery on a certain linendraper, who had only to wait for the death of Blondeau, its originator. But as the draper was void of any skill outside his own trade, the grant was whittled away when the time came. The salary of £100 was duplicated; one salary went with the work to the Provost of the Moneyers; the draper received the other. Newton shied at a double payment which had already run for years, and stopped the Provost's money at the end of March 1701. But as the draper remained incapable, the Treasury sanctioned both salaries on the Moneyers' appeal against the decision.[4] The rule that all coin dies should be destroyed at the year's end had been neglected; the Mint was now searched and all out of date dies, of which over 100 were found in the Roettiers' house, were formally defaced in presence of the Board

(1700).[1] But Newton, buying for £5 out-of-date dies of Symonds, Chief Engraver during the Commonwealth, that had been taken from the Mint, caused them to be preserved as models for training the new entry (1701).[2]

It was probably also in 1700 that he restored the old strict accuracy to coining practice.[3] The definitions of weight and fineness of coins included certain tolerances, in Mint parlance the 'remedy'. So long as they were within the remedy, the coins could issue, and as weight had only to be a correct average on a pound of coin taken together, check on this point was very loose indeed; but the tradition of the Tower Mint, unlike some abroad, was to aim at the greatest exactness and take no optional advantage of the remedy. This ideal had been dimmed. 'When I first came to the Mint,' wrote Newton, 'and for many years before, importers [*sc.* persons who brought bullion to be coined] were allowed almost all the remedy, and the money was coined unequally, pieces being two or three grains too heavy and others as much too light, and the heavy Guineas were called "Come again Guineas" because they were culled out and brought back to the Mint to be recoined (as was the common opinion).'[4] The caution of 'as was the common opinion' may be noted, since Newton himself estimated that one guinea in eight 'came again', and admitted that it might be one in four. As to the duration of lax practices, on second thoughts he reduced 'many years' to 'some', and on third, he cut the phrase entirely out. 'Many years' was probably right enough, for assays

1 *British Numismatic Journal*, 1911, p. 258.

2 Warden's Accounts.

3 It was after 16 February 1699, when the guinea was reduced to 21*s.* 6*d.* and before the latter part of 1701, when Newton MSS. ii, 616 was written.

4 Newton MSS. i, 248, 250.

of the guineas received for the gold recoinage of 1774–77 show inferior fineness in the reigns of Charles II and James II (1660–88), an improvement in that of William (1688–1702) and a further improvement in that of Anne (1702–14). Newton, as will appear, overstated the fineness of gold in his current assays, and so failed to come quite up to standard. He also insisted, and there seems never to have been a fresh relapse by the Mint, that the individual coins should be struck very nearly to their exact weight; for which purpose he laid down limits of individual variation, a little wider than those to which the average had to conform, and proportionately more for small coins than large. As a grain of gold was worth $2d.$, culling importers lost an average profit of $2\frac{1}{2}d.$ to $5d.$ per ounce of gold coins struck for them, and the average weight of coins entering circulation was raised in the same measure. The change in fineness, by putting more gold into each guinea, resulted in a fall in the Mint value of gold from £4. 0s. 2d. to £3. 19s. $8\frac{3}{4}d.$ an ounce. For future coinage and for foreign exchange it was equivalent to keeping the old standard and reducing the face value of the guinea by $1\frac{1}{2}d.$ These alterations Newton made on his own authority.[1]

Silver bullion was again plentiful enough in 1700 for Parliament to be moved to undo two hindrances imposed on the manufacture of plate at the start of the Great Recoinage. The immemorial sterling standard of fineness had been replaced by the higher but more difficult and less practical Britannia standard; and the power to hall-mark the new plate had been limited to the Goldsmiths' Hall in London. The Mint naturally opposed an easement that meant more silver for plate and less for coin; Newton gave his evidence in the House of Commons against both

1 Hopton Haynes, 'Brief Memoires of the silver and gold coins of England...1700', Brit. Mus. Lansdowne MSS. DCCCI.

changes (4 April 1700), and succeeded in averting return to the sterling standard.[1] It was again proposed and resisted by Newton in 1715, and was effected in 1719.[2] The rest of the fight was lost. New hall-marking Companies were sanctioned in each town where had been a temporary Mint,[3] with reversion of its premises; Newcastle was added next year.

As old hall-marked plate had been found by the Mint to be below standard, Newton drafted and secured a clause to keep the new bodies up to the mark; it bade them set aside a few grains from all silver work passed, and, on a request by the Lord Chancellor, send this 'diet of the plate' once a year to the Mint to be tried by the jury that judged the coin. He failed to carry a further provision that if this was not done for two consecutive years, the diet should go to the London Goldsmiths for examination.[4] Consequently, as the Lord Chancellor only issued his rescript in a single year, 1707,[5] the clause remained inoperative and the Assay Halls immune from scrutiny. But its intention was later approved, for when other Halls were created at Birmingham and Sheffield in 1773, submission of their diets for examination by the Mint itself was made compulsory.[6] And on a review in 1889 the only survivor of the older Provincial Halls was brought into line.[7]

Early in 1700 Newton challenged, on very technical and almost antiquarian grounds, the assessment of his property at Twyford to poor and highway rate. He pointed out that Twyford, though situated in the Parish of Coulsterworth which lay in the Soke of Grantham, was not considered to be itself in that Soke. And so the property was seemingly

---

1 M.R. 7, 2; Luttrell, iv, 631.   2 Wrought Plate Act, 1719.
3 Britannia Standard Provincial Offices Act, 1700.
4 Newton MSS. ii, 249.   5 Ibid. i, 237.
6 Sheffield Assay Act, 1773.
7 *Mint Annual Report for* 1889, p. 64.

assessable, if by any one, by the Constable of Coulsterworth alone, and certainly could not be assessed, as was
purported to have been done, by the Constable of Witham
and the Justices of Kesteven.[1] Which no doubt was
perfectly true.

He continued to act as Treasurer or Auditor till at any
rate the end of 1700 of the Thomas à Beckett Charity, the
Tabernacle, Golden Square; for the accounts for the last
quarter of the year were prepared by him.[2]

Uneasiness persisted about money organisation generally
and the shrinkage of silver coin in particular. Mr John
Pollexfen, Member of Parliament, Member also of the
Board of Trade, and an energetic economist, published in
1697 a criticism of monetary policy, which was republished
in 1700.[3] 'It being the business of the Officers of the Mint
to preserve and increase the coin of this Kingdom',[4]
Newton, after long cogitation, examined these criticisms,
apparently for the Board of Trade, during that year; as
the author defended his views, a second examination
followed next year.

The foundation of Newton's attack was statistical. He
had no use for his opponent's 'general way of arguing
without coming to a reckoning'[5] that is, to figures, on some
points; while on others he found bad mistakes in the figures
used. The Mint's output of gold and of silver coin year by
year was on record back to 1660; it could be estimated also
to the beginning of Elizabeth's reign. Breaking the figures
up into periods of constant trend, Newton married the
variations between the stages to international events, and
deduced that falls in average coinage were caused by a

---

1 Newton MSS. ii, 628.   2 Ibid. ii, 642; Sotheby, 308.
3 John Pollexfen, *A discourse of Trade, Coyn and Paper Credit*, 1697,
reprinted 1700.
4 Newton MSS. ii, 584.   5 Ibid. ii, 621.

state of war or changes in economic relations; and at any rate not by the growth of the use of paper instruments, like Exchequer bills, Bank credits, notes and so on; since whatever change these brought about must be gradual and consistent.

The conclusion was false. William III's French war, the vital period, produced in the words of a modern economist the 'first credit inflation'.[1] Of the causes at work Newton isolated one, War; Pollexfen, another, Paper. But Newton had taken in his stride a novel position. It was not then so obvious as it seems to us that gold coin could not be disregarded; Locke had deemed it no more than convenient merchandise; the Bank of England had deplored large imports of gold; Pollexfen had omitted such coin from his reckonings except by mistake. A couple of years before this controversy, an opponent of the reduction of the guinea to 21s. 6d. apologised for heterodoxy: 'I must affirm (whatever some do urge to the contrary) that gold coins are money as well as silver.'[2] Newton, in his argument, set gold on equality with silver coin.

To drive his point home, Newton estimated that in the difficult years between 1689 and 1700, metallic circulation had only dropped £2,650,000;[3] the fact that silver, which alone was real money for most people, had fallen to one-half he passed in silence.

Leaping another century ahead, Newton's imagination ran on to propound his theory of a managed currency. He said in effect that it did not matter whether the money of the country were paper, backed by good security of a sound Government, or gold or silver, provided that there was

1 Feavearyear, op. cit. pp. 109 ff.
2 Anon. 'A Third letter to a Member of Parliament concerning the value of guineas and a true proportion between gold and silver.'
3 Newton MSS. II, 131.

enough metallic currency to pay taxes and enough silver
coin for 'market money and workmen's wages'.

'Tis mere opinion that sets a value upon money; we value it
because with it we can purchase all sorts of commodities, and
the same opinion sets a like value upon paper security.... All
the difference is that value of gold and silver is set upon their
internal substance or matter and therefore is called intrinsic,
and the value of paper security upon the apparent form of the
writing and therefore called extrinsic, and that the value of the
former is more universal than that of the latter.[1]

If total currency was not enough to allow full employment,
it should be expanded by creation of more paper; against
that, the total should not be let rise to a level that caused
'luxury' imports to increase, and bullion to be exported.
An adequate total circulation was revealed by a high rate
of interest; while low interest rates showed that it was
excessive.

If interest be not yet low enough for the advantage of trade
and the designs of setting the poor to work...as diverse under-
standing men think it is not...the only proper way to lower it
is more paper credit.... Let it be considered therefore what
rate of interest is best for the nation and let there be so much
credit (and no more) as brings down money to that interest.[2]

And again:

So much [sc. paper credit] is best for us as suffices to lower
interest, make dispatch in business, set the people on work, and
inspire life and vigour into the busy part of the nation; and
more than this may be of ill consequence by inclining the
nation too strongly to luxury....[3]

What that rate should be would have to be determined by
Parliament or experience or the Board of Trade.

1 Newton MSS. II, 631.   2 Ibid. II, 608.
3 Ibid. II, 614.

This advanced view was a flash in the pan; Newton for the future treated coined bullion, and in the end coined gold, as the sole real money. He frankly admitted now that there was no remedy for the gradual supersession of silver coin by gold. It was an inevitable consequence of the Chinese and Japanese esteeming silver twice as dearly as Europeans in proportion to gold:

Our silver must go to China till gold is dearer there or cheaper with us. And it is our interest to let it go thither. For China is inclined to take off our manufactures which India is not, and therefore is fit to be traded with and the trade for their gold must greatly increase our coin, being a profit to the nation as to the merchant himself.[1]

As some corrective, he advocated making an end of the rivalry between the two great exporters of silver, the old and new East India Companies, by division of the East into two spheres of trade and not, as others wished, by their coalescence into one overpotent corporation. As usual with his ideas, the Government thought otherwise. The Companies were amalgamated in January 1702.

During his Pollexfen controversy, Newton dealt with two concrete coin problems. The French gold Louis, and the similar Spanish gold pistole, had been imported in great quantities and were circulating at 17s. 6d. each. In January 1701 he wrote to the Treasury that, compared with the 21s. 6d. guinea, the gold in these coins was only worth 17s. 1d.[2] The Mint drafted a proclamation[3] to lower the aliens to this value, but during the next ten days, while the Treasury hesitated over a one-sided discount for their loss by wear, the Master had a lot of fresh assays made, and

1 Newton MSS. II, 308.
2 S. Dana Horton, *The Silver Pound* 1887, p. 261.
3 M.R. I, 204.

brought the value down to 17s.[1] Reduction to 17s. was proclaimed[2] and had the result, apparently quite unexpected, that £1,400,000 worth of gold Louis were rushed to the Mint to be turned into guineas.[3] The Board had to sit an extra day a week to meet the pressure.[4]

Newton had taken the opportunity to warn the Treasury that silver coin was being melted down and exported wholesale, and that tender of silver bullion for coinage had ceased. It was worth more as bullion than as coin. On an alteration in the French ratio between gold and silver coin, announced on 17 September 1701, he returned to the charge with a question whether the 21s. 6d. of the guinea should be reduced. The Treasury told him to go into it more thoroughly,[5] and he made a comprehensive study during the next nine months of the coins of Europe up to the Russian frontier, though American irregular silver, Turkish and even Scots money, crept temporarily into the net. The research extended into the queer names and the methods of reckoning of the several States, their rates of exchange and the cross exchanges over Amsterdam, and, of course the weighing and assaying of many individual specimens, struck sometime within a century back. He appears to have bought a large number of these with his own money; when he died, a packet of them still lay in his house.

As much had been done by the Mint in Commonwealth times;[6] the papers had been impounded by the restored King, but Reynolds' little book[7] with its tables survived.

---

1 Newton MSS. ii, 148.
2 Order in Council of 5 February 1701 (H. of C. 135 of 11 March 1830).
3 Report of 25 August 1717 (Shaw, Writers).
4 M.R. vii, 23. 5 Horton, loc. cit. p. 263.
6 Shaw, Writers, pp. 87–113.
7 John Reynolds, *A brief and easie way by tables...to cast up silver and gold*, 1651.

Newton, however, preferred, though examining some of
the same denominations, to do all the work anew. His
quill filled quire after quire in version after version; when
all was finished and approved by the Board, he copied it
again, some thousands of words, rearranging and enlarging
his tables, in a single day, for transmission to the Treasury.
He evidently wrote with tremendous speed. The valuations
of foreign coin were much more meticulous, and no doubt
more accurate, than the old. But what with the aberrations
of assay methods and the variations of even newly issued
coin, it was futile to try to assess a denomination to a
fraction like a thousandth of its value. Where there was no
large change, Reynolds' 54d. for the Emperor's dollar was
plainer than Newton's 54·27d. What leaps to the eye, if
details are cut out, is that in the half century gold had risen
in comparison with silver about one-quarter in England,
but only about one-sixth on the Continent. This major
fact, so useful in argument for Newton's conclusion, was
overlooked.

That conclusion was that the guinea exchanged for
proportionately more silver than gold coin of foreign
countries, to the amount of about 10d. or 1s., and that it
should be lowered to either 20s. 6d., 20s. 9d. or 21s.
Approximation forced its way in at the end.

The report recommended reversal of the law on export
and import of silver, as it failed to keep up the stock of
coin. Silver bullion could be exported legally, if it was
declared to be of foreign origin, and so it stood at a higher
price than coin, which could not. For there was some little
risk and labour in gathering and melting down full weight
coin. It never paid now to turn silver bullion into coin;
but it paid at times to turn coin into bullion. Newton
proposed that tally should be kept of all imports of silver
and that export should be freely allowed of an equal

amount of either metal or English coin, to earn interest, while awaiting export, and thereby increase the circulation. The expense of coinage was to be met by a levy on the exported money. Newton was keen enough on his plan to draft a complete Act of Parliament,[1] a couple of months before the completion of his report, to embody every detail. It was a good scheme for a frictionless world, but confined the external trade in silver of England and Ireland to the Port of London, left Scotland as an open gate, and assumed that the merchant could always get back coin of full weight for export.

Finally, the report rejected tersely the Treasury suggestion that the silver content of coinage should now be reduced or its face value increased. A discarded draft contemplated reduction of fineness to a round eleven-twelfths, like gold, because exchangers forgot the excess over this figure, but with corresponding increase of weight. A coarser silver and increased size was definitely recommended for small coins only, and it was suggested that copper coinage might extend to the penny. This last was done in 1797; the Mint soon resumed its objections to combining different standards of silver in a coinage. Neither proposal was new; in the 1695 discussions 'a merchant' had recommended inferior silver or base metal for all coins below sixpence 'for it is no great matter what metal such small exchange money is made of'.[2]

The report[3] was signed on 9 July 1702, after war with France had been declared and as a general election was returning a House of Commons wholly Tory. It was put in a pigeon-hole.

An Irish rumpus demanded political tact. Since the

---

1 Newton MSS. II, 576.   2 Goldsmiths' Library, Vol. 62.
3 Printed in Shaw, Writers, pp. 153–69.

brief, inconstant Mints of Ireland flickered out two centuries before, the Pale had been wont at times of turmoil to call for a Mint in Dublin. It was granted after the Restoration, but the grant was cancelled forthwith on the protest of the Mint in the Tower. The petition was repeated after the Revolution, and a Dublin Mint, coupled with a demand for separate and lighter Irish currency, became one of the slogans of a revived Home Rule Party. The London Mint defeated it for a time in 1693.[1] The Board in which Newton was Warden bludgeoned a second appeal in 1698 in violent and opprobrious terms.[2] Now, in 1701, being Master, and having to deal with a third approach, Newton steered for a compromise in language of careful courtesy.[3] How he had studied the political background is shown by a précis in his hand of Molyneux' book;[4] perhaps for that reason, the disadvantages to England of an Irish Mint are but darkly hinted at, as a thing too high for mere Mint judgement. The emphasis is on the importance of uniformity of coin, the costliness and infirmities of small mints. And so the letter leads up to the compromise of a temporary establishment for a year or so to convert to English money the foreign coin in circulation in Ireland. To such, the Tower Mint, that three years before had refused any truck with a rival, would give all possible help. Lest the official communication which he had got through his Board might read too grudgingly, Newton followed it with a personal letter to the same end.[5] Uniformity he no doubt asked for in all good faith, but as the English shilling stood at thirteen pence in Ireland, and the Irish wanted besides to make a profit, it was enough to

1 Try.pp. xxviii, 65.   2 Newton MSS. ii, 216.
3 Ibid. ii, 212.
4 William Molyneux, *The case for Ireland being bound by Acts of Parliament in England stated*, 1696. Newton MSS. iii, 456.
5 Newton MSS. ii, 222.

quench Dublin zeal. At any rate, the project died without need of the half measure.

This summer of 1701 saw a good deal of other departmental business. In May a Mr Samuel Davis proposed that the famine of small coin in the West Indies and mainland Colonies of America should be relieved by striking for them bronze coins of distinctive designs, a separate design being assigned to each of the four main zones; that the coins should be half the weight of English base-metal currency, which would have made them the size of modern English bronze; and that he should have one-third of the profits.[1] Newton adopted (9 July 1701) the idea of four currency areas with distinctive coins, but held, as he was to believe to the end, that small coins should be of pure metal, though it was but copper, and should be struck by the Mint of the fullest weight that its local value would admit, without loss but without profit to the State after payment of cost of coinage and distribution.[2] On that basis he recommended an issue of such amounts as the several Governors agreed upon; but nothing came of it, perhaps because the profit motive was lacking. The first and only issue of distinctive copper coin for that part of the world was £1,400 of halfpence made by the Mint for Virginia in 1773.[3] They were about two-thirds the current English size.

On 6 August 1701 Newton had to undergo the first Trial of the Pyx of gold and silver coins made in his Mastership, and of those made in Neale's last six months. Annual before the Civil War and after 1870, the ancient ordeal was held during the intervening 230 years whenever the Mint chest was full or it suited the convenience of the Master. There, the average weight and fineness of samples

---

1 Try. pp. LXXV, 13.   2 Newton MSS. II, 403.
3 Mint Catalogue, I, 302; Select Committee on the Mint 1837 (App.), p. 222.

that had been set aside from each bag of coin were checked by a Jury of the Company of Goldsmiths, named by the Company and summoned by the Lord Chancellor with representative Peers of the Privy Council and certain legal officials. Writs had to be issued to them all, and to the custodians of the Trial pieces and the Exchequer weights and to the Mint itself.

It was customary for the Mint to brief the Lord Chancellor; Newton spent £10. 15s. on copies of precedents to make certain of absolute regularity, and himself wrote out the various writs and a synopsis for his Lordship.

The Mint clerks next made forty or fifty copies of a schedule of the coinage since the last Trial and of the coins in the Pyx Chest. The chest, schedules, Mint Indentures and other documents, and enough coal for the assay fires, were rowed to Palace Yard on the Trial day in the Mint barge by its two liveried boatmen. The Master and his colleagues arrived with this gear at nine in the morning; the Lords turned up an hour later; the Lord Chancellor made his ceremonial oration on the solemnity of the occasion and swore the Jury in; after a little comparison of the material, the great men went away, and left the goldsmiths to weigh and analyse under Mint surveillance. It was already old custom that the Mint should stand the Jury a dinner after their verdict, commonly at 'The Dog', hard by. The richness of the banquet may be judged from its cost. £1 a head was allowed for six Mint officers, but £2 each for jurymen. The ordering of the dinner was entrusted in practice to the Prime Warden of the Livery Company, who paid the bill and recovered from the Mint. The Mint, on plea of poverty, was recouped in turn by the Privy Purse till 1712.

How far patronage had shifted from Crown to Executive was shown on a vacancy in one of the autonomous control posts. The Weigher and Teller had been appointed by the King to guard the community against the issue of light coin, and merchants who brought bullion to be coined against any cheats by the Master. Newton was now asked by Ministers to choose the new incumbent. He nominated (5 September 1701) out of five applicants, mostly men in or about the Mint, one Hopton Haynes, a pretty constant employee from just before the Revolution till two years ago (1699), for his steadiness and readiness, good humour and good calligraphy, and all-round abilities. It 'is my interest', he pointed out, that the Weigher should please the customers of the Mint.[1] Formal appointment by a Privy Seal Warrant followed in due course (27 November 1701).

Mutual compliments suggest a personal friendship. Haynes was a Unitarian—a creed to which Newton was sometimes thought to incline—and of so firm a cast that he gave up his meeting-house rather than abandon the dramatic gestures of dissent with which he upset even its services.

Thus, in defiance of the strictures of a Select Committee and the Conformity Acts, the Mint appointed a Nonconformist to a key post and they still sheltered a Roman Catholic, for, though they had taken the coinage dies from old James Roettier, the engraver, they had let him keep his house.

Haynes was something of an author. A bulky history of the recoinage was finished soon after his appointment. Later he wrote a defence of the privileges of Mint personnel, an account of St Peter ad Vincula, the Chapel Royal in the Tower, and various efforts in theology. He translated into Latin Newton's two essays on texts in St John and Timothy. He acquired a Tellership in the Exchequer before 1714, and in 1723 Newton advanced him to King's Assaymaster.

1 Newton MSS. 1, 111, 112–6, 121.

CHAPTER IV

ART

THE succession of Anne on 8 March 1702 inducted Newton into the field of art. The Mint had to provide new coin designs and produce a coronation medal. After he had obtained authority to continue William's coinage for a time, Newton's first task on that head was to dig out former Warrants and other communications back to 1662,[1] that formal procedure might be perfectly followed. He made some experiments in drawing various arrangements of the new Queen's monogram,[2] but otherwise he seems to have forwarded the actual designs as he received them from the Chief Engraver's hireling, Croker; they were not entirely acceptable, and word came back to replace the Lion of Nassau, in the centre of the gold reverses, by a rose and not by the monogram, and on the obverses to cover with drapery the Queen's neck which had been left bare.[3]

The Master showed a scholarly interest in medal design. The drawing for the Coronation Medal was supported by an erudite, if laboured, exposition of its mythological symbolism. One may doubt whether a committee of statesmen was likely to be moved by the accumulation of quotations from Ovid, Nicander, Philostratus, Isacius, Q. Smyrnaeus, Virgil, Flaccus Argonauticus and St Matthew.[4]

A few months later, he drew with his own hand the lay-outs of a dozen alternative inscriptions as they would

1 Newton MSS. III, 281.　　2 Ibid. III, 340.
3 Ibid. III, 282.　　4 Ibid. III, 289, 291, 292.

be presented on a pair of medals in honour of the expulsion of the French from the Meuse valley and of the destruction of a Spanish convoy in Vigo Bay,[1] with rudimentary sketches of other parts of the designs. One of these, intended for a medal to cover both the Meuse and Vigo victories, is a roughly sketched astronomical figure, depicting a luminous body revolving round the sun; no doubt Spain drawn into the orbit of France.[2] Two of his inscriptions were accepted, but with modifications; other subject-matters were preferred.

The success at Vigo Bay brought a little grist to the coining mills; the Mint was allotted so much of the treasure taken as would not sell, with instructions to put Vigo on the resultant coin.[3] But the whole only came to £13,342[4] in silver coin, with some gold, out of a capture valued at 700,000 dollars, or over £150,000. The Mint was able to smother various proposals to turn into halfpence or medals the captured cannon, which were the wrong calibre for the English Navy.[5]

The next of these unofficial medals, sold by Croker to celebrate the capture of Bonn, Huy and Limburg, in 1703, was attacked by party pamphlets for undue flattery of Marlborough. It depicted the surrender of the three cities as tendered to a solitary horseman. Newton had to defend it; he explained that the cavalier did not represent Marlborough, as the books still say, but stood for any small armed force, the victories having been cheaply won, and that the issue was the engravers' right, and did not commit the Government.[6] But, as sharp conflict raged, even within the Government, over the land war and its great leader,

1 Newton MSS. III, 305.   2 Ibid. III, 288.
3 Ibid. III, 277.   4 Ibid. II, 245.
5 Proposal of Samuel Proctor 1704; M.R. 46, 47; of Eyres, Newton
    MSS. II, 344.
6 Newton MSS. II, 312.

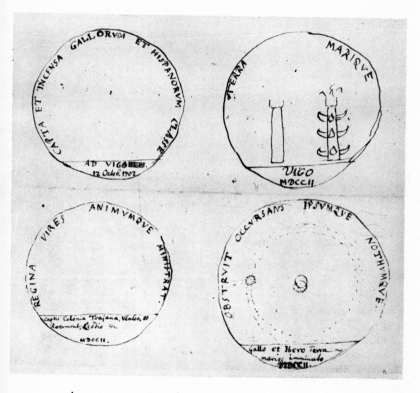

NEWTON'S SKETCHES FOR MEDALS ON THE VIGO AND MEUSE
VICTORIES.

Newton MSS III. 305.

semi-official medal-making was throttled down by the requirement of Treasury approval of all future designs.

The artist staff of the Mint had fallen low. The beauty of coins depended on the engravers. They originated designs; cut a matrix or master die for the main obverse and reverse of each denomination; sank a puncheon therefrom; the small separate puncheons for each letter and figure of the inscriptions were also carved by them. The heavy work of making working dies was done by the smith, the dies being retouched by the engravers. They also designed and struck the occasional commemorative medals at a small fee for each. Decoration of fighting forces was rare till the Napoleonic wars. They had the right of selling replicas, which they struck in copper as well as in precious metal, for their own profit; the right also, and if the King's effigy was used, commonly the monopoly, of striking other medals on their private account.

Of the forty medals struck in the Mint during Newton's Mastership, only the two Coronation Medals and the Peace Medal of 1713 were official creations, presented to Parliament, the Court and the Diplomatic Corps; the rest were made, usually in three kinds, gold, silver and copper, and sold for the profit of the engravers.

The Great Seal, the other English Seals and the Seals of the several Plantations and West Indies, were cut by an entirely separate expert, formally appointed for life, but without salary and paid so much a seal.

The three Roettier brothers had been recruited by Charles II personally in 1661 and given the joint appointment of Chief Engraver. They treated it as an hereditary estate; when two of them moved to Mints of France and Holland, their work was tacitly transferred to nephews; craftsmanship became a family preserve. In 1690 a duplicate post of Chief Engraver was conferred on Henry

Harris, hitherto the maker of seals, but, when time and politics had reduced the Roettiers to one crippled old man, it was found that Harris could neither 'emboss nor punch nor draw'[1] coinage or medal dies. Accordingly Harris hired a German jeweller, Johann Croker, in 1697 to do this work on his behalf, for a moiety of the salary when promises would no longer do. All Queen Anne's coins and medals were designed by this half-pay employee.[2]

When Harris died on 3 August 1704, Newton reorganised the engraving branch. Seal cutting, as 'no part of the constitution of the Mint', was again relegated to a separate unsalaried post, for which he chose William Roos, or Rosse, on the strength of his Duchy of Lancaster Seal. In order that the coin and medal work might never again fall to a cutter of seals, the cadre of the other engravers was fixed at three, with an obligation to train juniors and apprentices to succeed them.[3] As there was not work for three, and 'good graving is the best security of the coin', Newton, to keep their hands in practice, recovered for them—though it took till August 1706—the right of private trade in medals 'with plain historical designs and inscriptions in memory of great actions', subject to his approval of the designs and prices. Another condition was that the private work should be distinguished from the official by signature or initials.[4] Engravers continued to sign or initial both. The three posts were filled by Newton, in fact though not in form, after review of the qualifications of other candidates, with Croker, who was later naturalised by special Act, Samuel Bull, who had been an apprentice since the recoinage, and Gabriel Le Clerk, then at work in the German Mint of Zell. This last never did a hand's turn

1 Newton MSS. I, 174.   2 Try.pp. IV, 25; LV, 12.
3 Ibid. XCI, 143; Newton MSS. I, 152, 158.
4 Try.pp. XCVIII, 508; M.R. 12, 60.

in the Mint. He made a short visit to England, asked leave
to see his parents in Germany, and thereafter flitted about
courts in that land. Newton had tried to postpone the
commencement of his salary to June 1705, as the money
was needed to repair the ravages of the Great Storm; he
was compelled by the Treasury to pay from midsummer,
1704, and to keep up the payments till 25 March 1709.[1]
First-hand German news was valuable.

The two medal engravers of Newton's time were in-
herited by him from the previous régime and his new
system bred no first-rate artist till the rise of the Wyon
family.

To complete the story, the smith and die-sinker was, as
it were, disestablished in 1710 and put at the mercy of the
Master, because the last holder, in Newton's words 'imposed upon me and behaved himself to me with great
insolence'.[2] The post had for generations been united with
the charge of cannon manufacture in the interior of the
Tower; the holder also, besides his die work, contracted
on terms for all metal work about the Mint.

There are few further records of Newton's intervention
in design. Three drawings by Croker for the Union with
Scotland Medal, 1707, were submitted by him to the
Government, which refused alike that which he recommended and the two he forwarded 'for variety'.[3] On
occasion, he canvassed others, including the versatile
Hopton Haynes, for suggestions[4] but a number of other
subjects, which had no better luck, for the Coronation
Medal of George I, may have been his own ideas; they
referred to the King's Protestantism, so he wanted to add
to the King's title, 'Defender of the Faith' brought up to

1 Newton MSS. 1, 166; Master's Accounts.
2 Newton MSS. 1, 223.   3 Ibid. III, 303.
4 Ibid. III, 309,

date by 'of Protestants'—'Fidei Protestantium Defensor'.[1]
With some such object the unamended title was indeed
put upon the coins for the first time, without change from
the form adopted by Henry VIII as Defender of the older
faith. And it was in vain that he pressed for the crowded
quarterings of the King's German arms to be simplified
to fit the narrow compass of the half-guinea and sixpence.[2]
This was probably a transmission of the artist's views;
what attention Newton paid to design was to content, not
form, to the idea expressed, not the aesthetics of expression.

1 Newton MSS. III, 330.   2 Ibid. III, 275, 283.

CHAPTER V

THE TIN TRADE

AT the end of 1703 Newton brought alien work into the Mint. The tin mines of Cornwall were the prerogative of the monarch, whose interest had hitherto been leased out for small payments. But the county was also rich in seats in the House of Commons. On Queen Anne's accession, Lord Godolphin, who had Cornish connections, bethought him that a different treatment of tin would bring in tamer members.[1] A contract was therefore concluded between the Queen and the Convention of Tin Miners, whereby all tin was to be sold to the Queen, who would buy, at a much improved price, 1,600 tons stannary, that is 1,714 tons avoirdupois, a year for seven years.[2] To secure a monopoly, it was also decided that she should buy, at the same price, the Devon output of 50 tons a year.

Newton heard that Craven Peyton, the Warden, with some subordinate Mint officers would put in for the management of the subsequent sales; he stepped in, during October, with an offer to undertake it at cost.[3] The low level of coinage permitted the 'Irish Mint' to be set aside for the storage of tin; rights to use the Ordnance quays and cranes for shipments in and out were negotiated; new staff were engaged and extra pay for old staff was fixed; equipment, scales and so on, bought; a system of accounts and checks devised; and rules for sales laid down. At home, these were simple; the merchant must take the blocks of tin as they came, without picking or choosing; he collected

1 Try.pp. xc, 22. 2 Newton MSS. iii, 520.
3 Ibid. iii, 476.

his purchase on the Tower quay, and was charged an unvarying price, calculated—if all the tin was sold—to equal the first cost plus transport to the Mint and all its handling and clerical expenses. Interest, rent and invisible expenses were omitted. The sale price remained a uniform £76 a ton, till 1714 at least, against £69. 10s. paid to the miners. They had previously received only £45.

Sales abroad, though smaller, took more thought. The price aimed at was that charged at home, plus the further expenses; but calculation was complicated by loss on exchange, undercutting by Dutch boats that took out tin in ballast, and other economies of private enterprise. Agents were appointed in Holland, Germany and Genoa; one of them was the great merchant, Sir Theodore Janssen, who obtained specially worthy paper for the second edition of the *Principia*. Newton had to decide what each market could absorb; whether it would support a salaried office; whether tin should be sold outright to an agent or through him on commission; and balance lower commission against willingness of agents to lend the Government money. He had also to settle the sporadic sales to a great range of uncovered places, including even India. Despite war and embargoes, indirect sales to France continued. Exports mostly sailed from the Tower; but a saving could at times be effected by shipping from Plymouth to the Mediterranean. The use of warships to avoid freight was called unfair by the Levant Company.[1] Sales at the Tower began in January 1704.

The new arrangements were only in their second year, and unsold stocks were already piling up, when one John Williams pressed the Government to raise the price, while a William Tyndale made proposals to increase both price and quantity. Newton saw each of the protagonists two or

1 Try.pp. cxxii, 59.

three times to convince them of their errors. Tyndale's idea was to strike tin money in denominations from £10 down to sixpence, of such weights that the indicated value could be realised by breaking up for metal, so that tin could change into coin and coin into tin without loss, like gold and silver. The ingenious propounder thought it an advantage that his coins of two or three hundredweight could not be passed easily from hand to hand, for a multiplicity of banks would thus be developed without hurt to the Bank of England. He forecast an increase of Crown revenue by £1,000,000 a year. Newton reported that the available tin was only £30,000 worth, and that it was already mortgaged for loans. Apart from that, the most objectionable part of the scheme seemed to him that the Exchequer was expected to accept the tin money for taxes.[1]

Williams' proposal was that the sale price of tin should be raised from £76 to £100 or £120 a ton, on the grounds that England held a monopoly of the metal, that tin was an essential material in many manufactures, and that it was employed in such tiny percentages that prices of the final product would scarcely move.[2] Newton launched inquiries far and near on the world production and consumption of the metal. These revealed a possibility, or more, that such a price would attract excellent tin in unlimited quantity from Siam and the Dutch East Indies. His agent in Holland sent a warning on general principles:

The driving of goods which several nations of the world afford up to a high price at one place generally proves the ruin of that place.... The English plantation sugars were kept up generally above 40s. to 56s. a hundred pounds in England, and above here; this has made the Dutch at Surinam, who never made above 5,000 hogsheads yearly, bring home 12,000 to 15,000 hogsheads for several late years, and, what has and is like to

1 Newton MSS. III, 578, 600.　　　　2 Ibid. III, 519, 534.

prove fatal to the English Plantations, is the Dutch East India Company have planted a great part of the Island of Java with sugar.

He added that these new sugars actually now fetched more than the English.[1] The proposal, but not the proposer, was defeated; he kept the correspondence up for two years more.

Newton's continual worry was that he could not sell anything like all the tin purchased. In this very year, 1705, sales being but 860 tons a year, he urged a large curtailment of purchases;[2] he repeated these representations in 1709, when they had risen to an average of 1,520 tons, and the contract was due for renewal,[3] and in 1714 when the contract was terminated by the Queen's death; average sales had then fallen to 1,260.[4] He pointed out on each occasion that the interest on the capital locked up entailed a loss to the Crown which he computed at some £200,000 by 1709; that the excess stock must be sold one day, and that its disposal, however cautious in order not to break the market, must depress prices and cause a further capital loss on the original price.

These reports read as if made for conscience' sake, without expectation of effect. The electoral drawbacks to diminished purchases were patent, and the renewed contract of 1710, a year of general election, promised an increased off-take of 200 tons annually as soon as the war ended, in the faith that peace would lift consumption.

In the new reign, rights in tin reverted to the Prince of Wales and Duke of Cornwall, whose interests were opposed to the Crown's; on 1 June 1717[5] the new management terminated the arrangements made under Anne, and this

1 Newton MSS. III, 577.   2 Ibid. I, 520.
3 Ibid. III, 487.   4 Ibid. III, 342.
5 Try.pp. LLXXXV, 17.

employment of the Mint. Newton for his part seems to have handed the work over to his Deputy Fauquiere a year or two earlier. Though the 'Irish Mint' was thus freed for the oncoming copper coinage, 'Queen's Tin' lay unsold in its cellars till well on in the 1720's, while the Treasury inculcated patience on creditors of her estate.[1]

1 Newton MSS. II, 439; Try.pp. CCVIII, 12, CCXVI, 3, CCXLIV, 34.

CHAPTER VI

LEIBNITZ AND FLAMSTEED

THE dissolution of 25 May 1702 ended Newton's membership of the House of Commons, without visible effect on the Mint. His lunar theory was published during the year by Professor David Gregory in *Astronomiae Elementa*.[1] A deal of unpleasantness ensued with Flamsteed who had furnished the data more than a lustrum before. In the autumn Newton went into the country to stay with Locke, who tried until next April to extort his criticism of an exposition of the Epistle to the Corinthians.[2] In the January of 1703 he had to unravel transactions of as long ago as 1697 by Anthony Redhead, then Deputy Master of Norwich Mint and now in gaol. Acknowledgements for £2,000 of hammered coin paid into the Norwich Mint were produced by a Mr Blofield, who demanded payment. After a lot of investigation and inference, it appeared reasonably certain that Blofield had been paid at the time, but that Redhead had carelessly accepted informal receipts in some cases and lost receipts in others.[3]

A little later, the Treasury sent him a conundrum created by the Tonnage and Poundage Act. This Act imposed a percentage duty to be calculated on net price realised less the amount of tax. The question was how such a computation could be made. After two examinations of the Act, a number of arithmetical and algebraic explorations, and three draft answers, Newton pointed out that for any given rate of duty, the tax could be expressed as a

1 More, pp. 332, 413. 2 Ibid. p. 489.
3 M.R. 8, 235.

lower percentage on the gross price, so that only one sum need be done by the Customs Officer.[1]

The Board of Trade asked through the Treasury, on 26 November, for sterling values to be made out for dollars, pieces of eight, ducatoons, crusadoes and French crowns, circulating in America, in order to get rid of the extraordinary variations between different Plantations. The Board had decided that the values must follow those already authorised by statute in Massachusetts, as new Imperial legislation would be too much trouble. Newton, however, retraced the ground in detail, and it was not till June that he produced a recommendation and draft Proclamation fixing on the Massachusetts basis maximum values which were 25 per cent above the valuation of the respective coins in England.[2] The men of the Plantations went their ways; the coins continued to pass in some above, and in others below, the proclaimed values. An Act had to be obtained after all, in 1707, to enforce uniformity; except in the Bahamas, no more attention was paid to it than to the Proclamation.[3] So much for Locke's thesis that a piece of silver, coined or uncoined, must be worth the same everywhere.

On the very night that the Board of Trade wrote about the Plantations, the Great Storm worked such destruction in the Mint that under the compartmented system of finance Newton had for years to scrape money from salaries to pay for repairs. At its annual meeting a few days later, the Royal Society elected him its President; it yearly conferred that honour and duty on him till his death. The Master's work, light for some years after 1703, was never so heavy as to preclude management of the Society's

---

1 Newton MSS. iii, 441, 446.
2 M.R. 7, 44; Newton MSS. ii, 17, 184.
3 Robert Chalmers, *History of Colonial Currency* 1893, pp. 13–15.

affairs or regular attendance at the weekly meetings. The new President, however, altered these from Wednesdays to Thursdays, as the former was the Mint's day for paying out coin. Newton presented his burning glass of seven lenses to the Society in the following January (1704); in February, the *Optics* was published; the only book of Newton's that he himself prepared for the press. It is not known whether it had long lain by in manuscript, or was newly compiled from old material. Newton continued to work on the subject; he gave the Reverend Samuel Clarke £500 for publishing a Latin translation in 1705; his fresh findings were added in the version published in 1718; and revisions were embodied in the third edition of 1721, and in the fourth, which was in the printer's hands at his death. There were bound up with the first edition two treatises, of which one, the *Tractatus de Quadratura Curvarum*, or computation of the areas circumscribed by curved lines, dealt with the author's discoveries, and the other, *Enumeratio linearum tertii ordinis*, classified a great number of curves.[1] The latter had been written 'many years ago'; the former was the first public exposition by Newton of his method of calculation by 'fluxions', and in a foreword he explained the reason for its publication:

In a letter written to Mr Leibnitz in the year 1676 and published by Dr Wallis, I mentioned a method by which I had found some general theorems about squaring curvilinear figures....And some years ago I lent out a manuscript containing such theorems and having since met with some things copied out of it, I have on this occasion made it public.

So were kindled afresh the flames of the famous controversy on priority in the discovery of the calculus. The framework of the basic facts has become clear. Among

1 Brewster, I, 348; More, p. 576.

other mathematical discoveries, Newton, in 1665 or 1666, 'fell into', to use his own words, the mode of calculation now called the differential and integral calculus, but by him dubbed fluxions. He spoke about it to certain of his friends; it is still disputed whether an essay which he wrote in 1669, *De analisi per series numero terminorum infinitas*, was confined to other mathematical advances or gave away the secret of the fluxions; Newton thought it did. Leibnitz visited London in 1673, read the *Analysis*, talked with those friends and kept up correspondence on mathematics with them during the next few years. In 1675 or 1676, Leibnitz also hit upon the calculus in a different terminology and a different notation, which the world at large has found the handier. He wrote to Newton twice in 1676 for information on the latter's methods; in reply to the iterated inquiry, Newton, on 24 October 1676 (the letter mentioned in the foreword to the *Quadratura*), recorded a summary of their nature in two jumbled anagrams or cyphers. Leibnitz sent a clear account of his own differentials to Oldenburg on 21 June 1677; in 1684 he published a paper upon them. Newton, on the contrary, after his habit said no more of the fluxions; he used them in exploring the problems of the *Principia*, but he demonstrated and proved the solutions entirely by the established geometrical reasoning. One scholium alone recalled his discussions with Leibnitz. In 1693 a brief account of the fluxions was published by Wallis, and a full text-book on Leibnitz' differentials appeared in 1696. When Newton solved the brachistochrone problem in 1697, Leibnitz boasted that the solution had been effected by his— Leibnitz'—differentials.

In fine, Newton had been the first by some ten years; Leibnitz probably knew no details of what he had devised, but he learned that a way of making calculations of the sort had been found, and that is more than half the battle; where one has gone, the road is known to be open. The first ascent of the Matterhorn cost many trials and several lives; afterwards ladies and even a cow reached the summit. But Leibnitz' system was the more practical; and it was handed out for general use.

Leibnitz reacted to the statement in the *Optics* in an anonymous review of the book in the *Acta Eruditorum* of Leipzig of January 1705. He vigorously denied authorship of the article; therein he was true to the first syllable of his name, for the manuscript signed by him has been found. In this review, he called himself the inventor of the calculus, described it, and went on: 'In place, then, of the differentials of Leibnitz Newton employs, and has always employed, fluxions—"Pro differentiis Leibnitianis D. Newtonus adhibet, semperque adhibuit, fluxiones;"—and has used them elegantly in the *Principia* [which was also untrue] and other works, in the same way as Fabri [a notorious plagiarist] modified the notation of Cavalieri.'

Newton did not reply; the cudgels were taken up on his behalf by lesser hands.

On 10 April 1704 Newton visited the Royal Observatory at Greenwich and launched those negotiations which procured the printing by December 1707 and ultimate publication in 1712 of Flamsteed's catalogue of star positions, the *Historia Coelestia Britannica*. He canvassed the Prince Consort on 7 December for the necessary funds; on 23 January 1705, he drew up the report of the editorial and management committee. Flamsteed wrote on 17 November that Newton had at last forced him to enter into articles for printing his works with a bookseller, very disadvantageous to himself.[1] Flamsteed rumbled and grumbled over the way he was handled, but it was Newton's

1 Brewster, II, 166.

management and drive as well as his solicitation of finance from the Prince, and after his death from the Queen, that got the work into print. But the world was little the better for it; Flamsteed put most of the copies into the fire.

Dies for marking documents with duty appear then as now to have been made in the Mint. This spring of 1705, Newton had referred to him an idea for excluding forgery by gluing a duty mark on the paper. After several interviews with the inventor, he reported the device to be useless, 'unornamental', liable to be counterfeited more than the die stamps, and likely to cost more than the Revenue lost by forgeries.[1] The inventor angrily protested that Newton knew not the first thing about stamps. Four years later, when the dies were worn out, Newton was asked to make new ones with some alterations of design which would render forgery more difficult. He could not agree on these with the Commissioners of Taxes, so repeated the old pattern, but passed on without enthusiasm a notion of one Rollos, who was later appointed Engraver of Seals, for stamping the documents between a die and a counter-die to obtain a deeper and less imitable impression.[2]

As a general election was in sight, the Queen took steps in 1705 to attract voters to the side which Godolphin favoured; one of these was to raise Newton to Sir Isaac at Cambridge on 16 April.[3] But in spite of this mark of Royal approval, and of the flowing Whig tide, his candidature for the University suffrages for Parliament was defeated next month. The honour led him to spend a good deal of time and money to get his pedigree established by the Heralds' College;[4] the Arms which they assigned him —sable, two shin bones saltire wise, the sinister surmounted

1 Newton MSS. III, 447.   2 M.R. 7, 56.
3 More, p. 522.   4 Ibid. pp. 2, 3.

by the dexter, argent—he had been using as a seal since at least 1693.[1]

That year, Newton assisted his old University in an educational duty that may have been more important to them than representation in Parliament; with others, he drew up the constitution of the new Plumian Professorship of Astronomy.[2]

The ebb of coinage had gravelled the Company of Moneyers, dependent as they were on payment by the piece; some of them had sunk to employment as casual labourers outside the Mint.[3] In similar distresses in 1693 the Treasury had bestowed salaries of £30 a year each on the Moneyers, until the recoinage set the Mint to work once more. Such departmental grants seemed to Newton informal, even *ultra vires*; a statute was therefore procured in 1706 to add £500 per annum to the limit on Mint standing expenditure, with effect from Christmas 1705. £100 of this was meant to improve the salaries of the Mint clerks, but urgent building repairs absorbed it for long years. The other £400 was given to the Moneyers for division, on condition that their numbers were steadily brought down to sixteen, who would thus get £25 a head. To enforce reduction, Newton unnecessarily stipulated for a veto on admission of apprentices; it remained unexercised until near the close of the century, when though the Moneyers were down to eight or nine, the threat of it was used by a couple of Masters to obtain apprenticeships for their friends. Gold coinage began to look up, as soon as the statute was passed; the allowance was withdrawn in September 1714, on account of the prosperity of the Moneyers, but it had to be revived again in 1729.

The year 1706 brought a little booty to the coining

1 Sotheby, 134.   2 More, p. 525.
3 *Royal Commission on the Mint*, 1848, p. 62.

presses. A pirate, Captain John Quelch, was captured by
the Navy off New England; Newton was instructed on
3 January 1706 to take over, and later by word of mouth
to coin, gold dust valued at £4,137. 15s. 9d., taken in the
ship. A Mint officer was sent down to Portsmouth to fetch
it; the dust was found not only to have been valued at the
Plantation rate of £5. 5s. an ounce, but to be mixed with
3 per cent of iron filings, which hampered its treatment.
So it produced only £3,164. 19s. 8d. in guineas of which
Newton won back twelve for his pains for the Mint
messenger, 'who in modesty would make no demand on
that account'.[1]

It was probably in April 1706 that Catherine abandoned
her uncle to cleave to Montagu, and sometime during the
year Whiston, his deputy and successor at Cambridge,
published, with leave or without,[2] his old Lucasian lectures.
They appeared in 1707 under the title of *Arithmetica
Universalis*.

In August the lawyers at last decided that the Mint's
freedom from all public duties, whether of Lord Mayor or
tax collector, did not excuse the Master from furnishing
two men for the Militia.[3]

1 M.R. 8, 55; Newton MSS. 11, 369. 2 Brewster, 1, 351.
3 M.R. 7, 9, 52.

CHAPTER VII

RECOINAGE AT EDINBURGH

THE TREATY reached in 1706 for the Union of Scotland with England became law from 1 May 1707 by an Act passed on 6 March. The terms of interest to the Mint provided for the continuance of the Edinburgh Mint under regulations to be brought into line with those in the Tower; for the introduction into Scotland for its support of those taxes on liquor on which the London Mint subsisted; and for the adoption by Scotland of English coinage. The last provision was taken to mean that native or foreign silver coin in circulation in Scotland should be converted in Edinburgh into English currency; the Northern coppers, which continued to circulate till at least 1738,[1] and gold coin were left to the mercy of time.

Newton got under way a fortnight after the passage of the Act. He saw the Lord Treasurer of England and the Earl of Seafield, architect of the Union on the Scottish side, and drafted a score of separate Warrants to authorise steps required. The Goldsmiths were moved to make new sets of Trial Plates of gold as well as of silver for both Mints; the Warden to fashion for both new sets of identical working weights; puncheons and dies identical with the English except for the Mint mark 'E' were put in hand for the silver coins from the sixpence up; and the Scots were asked for a list of machines and materials of which they were short; which list begat some bewilderment by what seemed to be Doric terms, but turned out to be clerical

---

1 Thomas Ruddiman, *Introduction to Mr James Anderson's Diplomatica Scotiae*, 1773, p. 232.

errors. An instance of restrictive monopoly comes to light. Cast iron had replaced wrought in rollers for mills; but cast iron rollers were not to be bought: 'the man who makes them keeps the secret to himself and only lends them to the Moneyers at 10s. a day.'[1]

Deeming identity of result to require identity of process to the last particular, Newton invited the Scots either to send men down to be trained in London ways or to accept, which they liked better, overseers from London. Three Moneyers, afterwards increased to four, agreed to leave 'their families and their farms';[2] one of the Master's clerks accompanied them for three months to bring the computation of pot charging and the records to a London footing. Further, Newton, who had attended to all this business personally, had Dr David Gregory, Savilian Professor of Astronomy at Oxford, appointed general supervisor for the same period of the initiation of the new coinage.[3] It was a nice return with a fee of £250 for the *Elements of Astronomy* in 1702. But the fairer explanation may be that Gregory was an Edinburgh man.

As in England in like cases, he also got a local commission set up to take in the old coin and melt it into ingots of known fineness before transfer to the Mint.[4]

The Professor reached Edinburgh on 1 August 1707, after eleven days on the road; the others arrived the same week. But some of the gear ordered in June was still at sea, and other essential machines had been overlooked by the Scots; these were now sent up by the land route, for speed.

Metallurgical practice in the Edinburgh Mint differed from the English. The melting furnaces were fired not with charcoal but with coal, which threw a fiercer and

---

1 Newton MSS. III, 72, 70. 2 Ibid. III, 175.
3 Ibid. III, 182. 4 Ibid. III, 130, 160.

wilder flame; and it took twice as long as in England to ladle the molten contents into the moulds. Meanwhile, the crucible stood on the furnace, slowly losing more copper than silver in the enduring heat. The Scots had been wont to add some grains of copper when the crucible was half emptied; this was stopped on Newton's orders as a divergence from Tower practice.[1] Charcoal was unobtainable in Scotland, and the other differences of technique had to go on.

The Moneyers naturally knew nothing of firing, and the Edinburgh Melter may have been out of practice; since 1701, he had only coined £4,500. At any rate, the castings of the next two or three months were not coinable. Newton posted empirical hints of his Melter on temperature control, and looked about for a skilled man for Edinburgh. However, that corner was turned; it was then found that though the first bar from a pot might be perfect, the last would have up to 931, instead of the sterling 925, thousandths of pure silver. Edinburgh took the bit in its teeth and restored the addition of copper, though in two instalments instead of one, and with more numerous check assays. Newton hesitatingly assented in view of the urgency of getting under way, with a stipulation that uniformity should again be attempted as soon as the recoinage was completed.[2]

Coining started in earnest at the end of October;[3] by 21 November, when Gregory went home, it had reached £6,000 a week.[4] It soon dropped; for half the nineteen months that the Moneyers stayed in Edinburgh, it failed to reach £1,000 a week.[5] The Bank of Scotland had none the less collected the whole of the sum recoined by the end of 1707; they had to disgorge some of the Scots coin next

1 Newton MSS. III, 181.   2 Ibid. III, 183, 187.
3 Ibid. III, 186.   4 Ibid. III, 173.
5 M.R. 8, 157.

March, when a Jacobite invasion threatened, to pay soldiers and keep the public at ease, but had regained it by the autumn.[1]

The London Moneyers were permitted to return in the middle of March 1709. They had struck in all only £320,372. 12s.,[2] the figure subsequently given for the Edinburgh recoinage in Mint Parliamentary Returns. In addition local men had produced without their supervision £2,723. 13s. 8d. during this period; and coined £398. 12s. 2d. later in 1709,[3] when plate was bought at a premium. These independent strikings may be the coins, long a puzzle to numismatists, which are picked out by a star after the Mint mark. Manifold questions poured on Newton during the recoinage. Extra clerks had to be allowed, and, more difficult, discharged when the work was done; existing staff to receive additional reward. The old Mint income was detained by its Collector, who, when he could refuse no more to give up the money, gave up the ghost, but left 'the men who do manage his children and successors' affairs' to find fresh grounds for not parting. The new taxes were levied very leniently in Scotland. Salaries went unpaid for half a year, at which 'there is like to be demur'. 'Upon the want of money for carrying on the business of the Mint', the Warden wrote to Newton, 'all the officers of the Mint depend on you very much in this matter...for the truth is that the Union has disconcerted our foundation entirely.'[4] The Edinburgh Master had to be advised how to wheedle cash out of the Treasury; the effort was best made, Newton thought, in October when the Lord High Treasurer returned from summer holiday. He had to be

---

1 Ruddiman, *Introduction to Mr James Anderson's Diplomatica Scotiae*, 1773, p. 231.
2 Newton MSS. III, 185.   3 Ibid. III, 31.
4 Ibid. III, 168.

told how to put items most acceptably in his accounts; what expenses must come out of his own share of the fees, or the Melter's or the Moneyers"; which, for instance, should pay for remelting light fillets, which the more economical Scotch practice had used up for smaller coin. At the end, he had to be shepherded through the Trial of the Pyx, which Lord Seafield had finally agreed should be held in London.

Newton disposed of these problems with thoughtfulness and tact. The great Earl of Seafield wrote 'as you have been at a great deal of trouble in directing this coinage and have done most justly to all concerned in it';[1] and again: 'I renew my hearty thanks for your former kindness. I depend upon your good offices in this new demand, and praying that the Lord may reward you for all....'[2] The high officers of the Edinburgh Mint were as profuse in their gratitude. It would be cynical to put it all down to cultivation of favours to come. Which in any case did not come.

This coinage past, the Scots started to heckle the English. An expenditure up to £1,200 a year had been proposed by the Edinburgh Mint and approved by Statute; the General of the Mint, a noble sinecurist above the Board, drew round sums from the allowance, as the spirit moved him, for the stipends which continued, work or no work, and the maintenance of his Mint. He was wont to append a request for a further advance 'outside the £1,200' for expenses of an actual coinage. The outlay on the Scottish Mint was now wholly subducted from the coffers of the sister institution; for customs duties on liquor were misliked in the North and were left uncollected after the first year or two of the Union. Newton responded with truth to the General's request that the £1,200 afforded a margin of £150 to £200, which would cover coinage, but could be

1 Newton MSS. III, 40.   2 Ibid. III, 36.

increased if need be by dropping his own useless post on a vacancy. He had for a while the further defence that the limit was statutory, but a new Coinage Act became due, at a time, soon after the accession of George I, when generosity to Scotch complaints was desirable. Newton himself proposed substantial additional allocations to the Northern Mint; the Act went further and cut out all separate limit on its expenditure (p. 105). The General could have had, then or earlier, any money within reason that he wanted, and as the charge for coinage was laid down by his Indenture, there could have been no dispute later on its propriety, Newton still stuck to his point that £1,200 a year was enough for needs. Commenting on the omission of the General to render any account for nine years past of his receipts and their expenditure, he tried to end the controversy in 1718: 'And that there may be no more complaints of the want of moneys to bear the charge of coinage, the said General may have notice to pay these charges in the first place and let the deficiency (whenever there be any) fall upon the salaries.'[1]

The General continued to sit on his accounts for five years more;[2] continued also his placid requests for a specific advance. They can have been but gestures to shift responsibility. Coinage of gold or of copper was never proposed. As for silver, the price doomed its coinage to a dribble that would have cost the Scots more than their extra fees. The Edinburgh staff continued their lives of ease, or other occupation, on full salaries, as in turn did their successors, without such horrid interruption; in 1709, the mills and presses of Edinburgh had been stilled for ever.[3]

1 Try.pp. CCXXV, 47; Newton MSS. III, 107.
2 Try.pp. CCXLVII, 22.   3 Ibid. CCXLIII, 32.

CHAPTER VIII

ALL KINDS OF VEXATIONS

THE London Moneyers were hardly back from Edinburgh, when, in April 1709, an effort was made to remedy the desperate scarcity of silver money in England. The Mint was granted £6,000 to pay an extra $2\frac{1}{2}d.$ an ounce during the next six months for plate or foreign coin; whence resulted a coinage of £78,811 in London, and one-two-hundredth of that figure in Edinburgh—in all, but half the coinage and half the expenditure contemplated.

Regular resources were at last provided by the same Act for measures against false coiners; £400 a year was allowed for their detection and prosecution; but detailed financial control of the new fund was vested in the Treasury—excessive and cumbrous centralisation against which Newton time and again protested; the expenditure under it averaged £250 a year.

The winter of 1709 brought a rare old-fashioned frost, which sealed up the Thames; it froze likewise the mains of elm under the Mint Street; carriage of water to the houses in pails and tubs cost an extra £2. 12s.

Next year, 1710, Newton, who had moved during 1709 from Jermyn Street to Chelsea, settled himself in a house on the east side of St Martin's Street.[1] He inspired and managed also the removal of the Royal Society to Crane Court from Gresham College which it had been in mind to quit since 1703. A good deal of umbrage was given to the Fellows by his determination and diplomacy in forcing a

1 More, p. 539.

decision by snap votes and packed committees.[1] His private purse contributed £110 towards the expenses.

The Queen was persuaded by him to appoint on 12 December 1710 a Board of Visitors under his chairmanship to inspect Greenwich Observatory;[2] more friction with Flamsteed was the fruit.

The gold Trial Plate superfluously made for the Scottish recoinage brought an aftermath of trouble. It was never used in Edinburgh, but the gold coins of the Tower Mint were tried against it on 21 August 1710. Thanks to new methods of refining, the Mint Assayer, from whom the Goldsmiths got their pure gold for blending in the plate, had supplied finer metal than ever before. When the customary proportion of silver was added in Goldsmiths' Hall, this superiority was preserved; the new plate contained 2·7 parts in 1,000 more gold than the previous one. Gold minting had continued since the last Trial in 1707 on the basis of the plate then in use, with which it was in fact in exact accord, but when the coins were assayed against the new standard of reference, they of course appeared defective. The Mint representatives seem to have protested with such vigour that they were ejected from the assaying chamber by the Goldsmiths. Disregarding demands for a modified form of verdict to bring out the Mint view, the Jury insisted on stating that the gold coinage was a quarter grain below standard, that is 2·6 parts in 1,000. Everyone appears to have known perfectly well what had happened.

Newton was very cross at the slur on the Mint. He argued that the business of the Jury was to ascertain facts in co-operation with the Mint officials, not to deliver *ex cathedra* judgements; and that pure gold was a conventional term. 'I am satisfied...that gold may be refined so

1 More, pp. 504, 505.   2 Newton MSS. ii, 334.

high as to be almost half a grain finer than 24 carats.'[1]
And again: 'The surest way to make gold just 24 carats
fine is to refine with antimony, then add pure silver in
such proportion as by experience is found to reduce the
gold to 24 carats.'[2] Twenty-two carat meant gold eleven-
twelfths as fine as gold so produced, and no more. Thus

> At the last Trial of the Pyx, the gold money was full standard
> by the Assay and the Trial piece $\frac{1}{4}$-grain better than the money,
> and the Jury in their verdict represented the money $\frac{1}{4}$-grain
> worse than the standard by the Trial piece. This Trial piece
> was made upon the Union 1707 A.D. It was made I think
> without an Order in Council and by many assays very carefully
> made is 5/12 grain better than standard. That of 1688 made by
> Order of James II is 1/6 grain better than standard and that of
> 1660 made by Order of K. Charles II is standard.[3]

The 1660 plate was in fact the poorest ever made in the
sterling standard, and only contains 912·9 parts of gold in
1,000,[4] instead of the 916·6 required. Newton calculated
correctly the superiorities of the other and of theoretically
pure gold, but missed the point that the 1707 plate really
was a shade too fine, for it contained 917·1 parts of gold in
1,000. Either there was a little gold in the alloy silver or
the Goldsmiths added too little alloy.

The wrongfulness of the verdict was manifest, Newton
protested, because, if it stood, the Mint would have to
work to the standard of the new plate, and comply with
the progress of invention; and the Goldsmiths would have
altered the coinage standard by their mere motion. So are
men deflected by a taunt from their courses as a bull by a
flaunted rag. Adoption of the 1707 plate would have put

1 Newton MSS. 1, 275.   2 Ibid. 1, 251.
3 Ibid. 1, 109.
4 *Mint Annual Report for* 1873, p. 89; Garbett's *Report, Select
    Committee on Mint*, 1837, Appendix, p. 219.

a pennyworth more gold into a guinea, and lowered the Mint price of gold in that proportion. Newton had himself reduced the price by three-halfpence a guinea in 1702 as a mere matter of office management and in 1702 and 1712 pressed the Treasury to knock off another 8*d*. or 1*s*.

The fuss which Newton made was effective. The plate of 1707 was never used again, and the gold coinage was in future tried against the 1688 plate till 1829. To be sure, the Mint at the next Trial, that in 1713, spent £91, in place of the customary £30 or so, on their dinner to the Goldsmiths.

Newton kept the gold coinage only a little better than the 1660 plate. After his death, the Mint advanced towards and finally up to the 1688 plate.[1]

The Earl of Godolphin, Lord High Treasurer thus far in Newton's Mastership, was deposed in 1710 by Harley, Earl of Oxford; who presently thought to match his predecessor's coinage by an offer of 4*d*. an ounce standard for plate, to be minted solely into sixpences and shillings. The higher price attracted no more silver than in 1709, but under the new Minister its passage through the Mint was less smooth. Newton was orally consulted before the project was ventilated in Parliament. He agreed to accept delivery of plate, and to give receipts for it by weight only, provided that a third party then took it over and melted it into ingots to be assayed. Thus there would be an independent record of the average fineness. 'For the Master is not to be entrusted with silver of uncertain value without due checks upon him.'[2] He was 'perplexed' to receive with no more said a Warrant of 1 May 1711 to give receipts in terms of price, coin the plate at speed into shillings and

1 *Mint Annual Report for* 1873, p. 89; Garbett's *Report*, loc. cit.
2 Newton MSS. II, 537.

sixpences and pay these into the Exchequer. As a pre-
caution, he drew up an alternative Warrant in which he
left blanks to force the Treasury to insert the proper names.
The Warden, Craven Peyton, 'fell into a passion' at the
blanks, and declined to take the document to the Treasury.
Newton amended the draft to meet Peyton's qualms, but to
cover himself prepared a third Warrant authorising the
Master to act on the second. This the Warden rejected
entirely; the new Warrant obtained on 10 May was a more
formal version of the first. The Mint had held back action
during the squabble about red tape; the pent-up plate now
poured in. The vendors were not paid; under a Resolution
of the House of Commons, the Mint receipts issued by the
Mint were to be accepted as cash subscriptions to a pending
Government loan. But the Treasury on the evening of
14 May wrote to the Mint that sellers of plate thereafter
must sign an acknowledgement that they did not expect
this privilege. A Resolution of the House confirmed the
privilege on the 17th, but no provision whatever was made
for sellers after the 14th in the Act, passed on 12 June and
published on the 19th. The miserable owners were de-
prived, apparently unintentionally, not only of their premium but of payment at the ordinary Mint price of 5s. 2d.
an ounce; for the coin from their goods had gone into the
Exchequer.

Newton tried to allay the storm. As the rest of the Board
would not concur, he made a series of personal representations to the Treasury. He ascertained quietly that the
merchants would be pacified by 5s. an ounce, with the rest
when Parliament reassembled, obtained the Attorney
General's advice that this was legal and drew up a Warrant
to authorise payment. In ordinary course a payment on
account was endorsed on a Mint receipt; the merchants
refused the suggested compromise when the Warden in-

sisted on surrender of the receipts in exchange for a fresh note of the remaining balance.[1]

The Lord Treasurer then, 24 July, called the officers of the Mint before him. Newton produced his sheaf of letters and the Law Officer's opinion. The Treasurer directed the Mint to pay all money outstanding, premium included, to persons who had sold them plate since 14 May. But as the premium could not be charged on Mint revenues, the Treasurer had to give the Board his written guarantee, first, that he would obtain legislation by Christmas to repay this excess to the Mint; secondly, that failing in this, they should be repaid out of the Civil List; and thirdly, that if he failed them in this also, Newton might take sufficient tin out of the storehouse and sell it during January.[2] So small faith was placed in the promise of a Prime Minister, but Lord Oxford got the legislation through in time.

The total coined was:

	£	s.	d.
From plate received from 10 to 14 May	45,603	2	8
From plate received after that date	25,908	19	8
	71,512	2	4[3]

With the usual dribblet from the Welsh lead mines, the whole coinage of 1711 was £76,780. 16s. Apparently it was all in sixpences and shillings.

It must have been in 1711, if ever, that an offer was made him of very handsome provision away from the Mint. Lord Bolingbroke, Secretary of State and Oxford's rival in the Government, it is said sent indirectly to Catherine Barton by the lips of Dean Swift a message that the Government thought he should be diverted from the Mint, in which case the Queen would settle £2,000 a year upon

1 Newton MSS. II, 539, 530.   2 Try.pp. cxxv, 36.
3 Newton MSS. II, 518.

him.[1] The post at that time was worth about £1,200 a year; the tenure was at pleasure, and it would have been easy for the politicians, had that been their wish, to dislodge an incumbent of sixty-eight in a year of confusion in Mint operations. No sane man would have entertained such an offer from a Bolingbroke, and if it was made, Newton rejected it vehemently.

Lord Oxford must have by now seen a good deal of Newton. When the Government decided to balance the growth of the chapels of dissent by the erection of fifty new churches in London and Westminster, he was appointed one of the commissioners for the project; at least he was one in 1717.[2] And in his private capacity, he supported the Church by subscribing to the Society for the Relief of Poor Proselytes.[3]

During all these years the War of the Spanish Succession had hardly affected the Mint except by restriction of coinage. The engravers had devised an almost annual medal to commemorate a victory by Marlborough; the Board had resisted demands for the support of the Militia; the staff had been protected from the Press-gang; and the last tin contract had envisaged the prospect of peace. It was as the war drew to its close that its currency problems were sent to the Mint.

The British Government borrowed 800,000 Mexican dollars for use in the Iberian Peninsula. They were to be delivered at Port Mahon in Majorca, shipped to Spain and there recoined on British account into Spanish two-ryal pieces. Newton was asked in June 1711 for advice on this last operation.[4] After computation of the original silver content of Mexican dollars, their probable degree of wear —on this he gave detailed instructions for weighing them

1 More, p. 452.   2 Newton MSS. II, 336.
3 Ibid. II, 106.   4 Ibid. II, 190.

on receipt, in presence of witnesses—the probable weight and fineness of a two-ryal piece, and the probable Mint charge in Spain, he reckoned that the Government should receive 4,200,000 of the Spanish coins. He recommended that these should be checked as to weight and fineness;[1] a single coin or pair of coins came home at intervals in the next six months for trial sometimes by him, sometimes by the Goldsmiths' Hall.[2]

In Marlborough's time, conundrums of foreign exchange as they affected the soldier had been decided without reference to the Mint. The English pay of forces in Flanders for example was issued to them in Dutch currency at a rate of conversion which was about midway between the pre-war and the commercial rate current at the end of the war. Marlborough was dismissed at the end of 1711, and when English troops occupied Dunkirk as the price of armistice a few months later, Newton was asked how much they should be given in foreign money.

Coins of half Europe were in circulation there. Inquiries into their value were begun, but had to be dropped; for the exchanges between the enclave and the hinterland had been cut. The exchange, however, for French livres was stated to be 17 livres to £1 sterling. As it took 19 livres 13·27 sous to equal in silver content 20s. of new English money, Newton recommended that, following the Netherlands precedent, the soldiers should be paid at a convenient round figure about halfway between the two rates. But he added that comparison of the theoretic metal par in the Netherlands with the war rate gave a larger loss by exchange, of which the Crown had borne only one-quarter: it was for Ministers to consider whether this were not the true precedent—and 17⅔ livres enough for the soldier's

1 Newton MSS. II, 143, 195, 209.
2 Ibid. II, 201, 209; Try.pp. CLVIII, 15.

pound.[1] The gap between the two solutions betrays the weakness of the diagnosis.

On 26 February and 2 June 1712 the Dublin Government asked the Mint through the proper channels to draft documents for them. Their Proclamations of 1701 and 1711, which appear not to have been submitted to the Mint, fixed a local value for certain foreign coins, including the pistole and its fractions but not its multiples. The Irish Courts consequently declared that counterfeiters who stuck to the higher values could not be prosecuted. Then the manuscripts of the Proclamation got burned, and the Courts refused to sentence any forger, unless the appropriate officer certified that the printed and published Proclamations were true copies, which that officer declined to do in the absence of the manuscripts. Newton, asked to redraft the missing documents, went on to criticise the values assigned to foreign coin by the Irish. He compared the bullion content of these coins with English silver and gold, allowed for the premium of a penny in the shilling which English silver coin held in Ireland, and for the like premium which he presumed prevailed for English guineas, and, using the broad brush and round figures, recommended that the gold moidore should come down from the existing 30s. 6d. to 30s. Irish, the silver crusado by twopence from 3s. 2d. to 3s.; and that to qualify for a value of 4s. 9d., the minimum weight prescribed for rix, cross and other dollars should be raised by 18 to 426 grains.[2] (The unworn weight of these was from 433 to 442 grains.) The first of these proposals was adopted; the other two, affecting the silver coins, and so annoying the man in the street, were rejected.

Newton took the opportunity to remind the English

1 Newton MSS. III, 161, 170.
2 Try.pp. cxxxvi, 39 (Shaw, Writers); Newton MSS. II, 236, 242.

Treasury that the guinea should be reduced by at least 9*d.* or 10*d.*

Into England also, Portuguese gold as well as wine of Oporto was poured by the Methuen Treaty of 1703; much of the gold was turned into guineas, and was the main raw material of the Mint for the last years of the war, but the moidore also circulated as it stood at 28*s.*, the equivalent of 30*s.* 4*d.* Irish. After the lapse of two years, in mid-1714, Newton advised the Treasury to reduce its English value by 6*d.* likewise, on the ground that moidores current in London were worth but 27*s.* 7¼*d.* as gold, and that those in the provinces, which took the more worn, were worth scarce more than 27*s.* 6*d.* So the Treasury by an order to all receivers of taxes to take the coin at that rate brought the moidore down to 27*s.* 6*d.* The reduction swept all the moidores into the Mint, and for the third time under Newton's management the country was unintentionally purged of a foreign coin. The West Country indeed petitioned that whereas their counties had been full of gold, the moidores were drawn now to London, as guineas had already been in great measure, to the detriment of trade and employment.[1] But no one headed their plaint.

To complete the tale of Newton's valuation of foreign coin for Ireland, he was asked in 1714 to value the new French currency of 1709, which was done without trouble, and in 1725 to assign values for a fresh Portuguese coinage of gold. He priced this series by comparison with the 21*s.* guinea at £3. 11*s.* 6½*d.* for its largest unit when in Mint condition, with proportionate figures for the smaller coins; but the true value for Ireland, which usually got worn specimens, he put at £3. 10*s.* These were English figures; the Irish premium would have raised even the higher of

[1] M.R. 7, 70 and Newton's Report of 21 September 1717 (Shaw, Writers, p. 194).

them only to £3. 17s. 6d. The Irish disregarded the recommendation, and fixed the value at £4, with the rest in
proportion. Presumably they would not risk loss of useful
currency by equating its face and its bullion value.

By 1713 the state of the coin produced in the Great
Recoinage caused some anxiety in England. In February
Newton and his colleagues were summoned to a Treasury
conference. Melting down of silver coin had become so
indiscriminate that some of the product was sent to the
Mint, at a loss, for recoinage. The coins had begun to be
clipped and the edges remilled. Loss of weight through
ordinary wear required attention. And counterfeiting of
copper coin had reached a scale to bother about. A further
report by the Mint was ordered. Newton investigated by
sample the amount of ordinary wear sustained by the new
coin, and the rate of wear to be expected by examination
of surviving old hammered coin. The rates were low compared with modern experience: about 1 per cent of the
original weight in fifteen years for a shilling.[1]

In January 1713 Daniel Brattle, the Queen's Assaymaster, died; he had obtained the post in succession to his
father, Sir John, one of the founder members of the Royal
Society, who had been appointed in 1665. The King's or
Queen's Assaymaster had, as his title indicates, for centuries been a technical and independent check on the
Master Worker. This distrust had vanished, and Newton
was left to choose a successor. He interviewed four candidates, and proposed a competitive practical examination.
The method was not new for Civil Service entries; it had
been adopted by the Customs a few years before; but
Newton admitted responsibility for the idea in this case.
Two of the candidates were frightened off; Charles Brattle,
brother of the dead Assayer, whom he had assisted for

1 Newton MSS. II, 83, 90; Conduitt, p. 46.

some time, and Catesby Oadham came before the Mint Board and performed a number of gold assays on 8 April 1713. The former was much more accurate in his results; his appointment was proceeded with; during its formal completion, Oadham appealed to the Lord Privy Seal, displayed his talents to the Earl of Yarmouth, organised a petition of protest by bullion merchants. Newton, though he quoted its results, did not think it enough to rely upon the competition; he pleaded that it was to his own advantage to have a competent Assayer; that this was also important to merchants of bullion; that only very small fry, who seldom sent a parcel, and that a tiny one, to the Mint, had complained; and that till substantial dealers did so, no one had a right to meddle with the Mint's choice. Then he turned on Oadham's character: he 'had neglected his master's business to mind Projects'; he had quit that business to sell stocks; 'not to mention his carriage to the Officers in such a manner as is not to be borne in an Assaymaster.'[1] The 'Projects', that is novel or speculative activities, rankled most. 'What is suspicious' about Oadham was 'that he designs not to be content with the Assaymaster's business but is projecting to make that post a step to something higher. Refining and assaying are manual trades and such trades are never closely followed by Projectors.'[2]

In the middle of this fret, the Mint was stung by the examiner of its accounts. Mr Auditor Harley, a brother of the new Prime Minister, had brightened his relative's triumph by a finding in 1711 that no less a sum than £23,000,000 was missing, strayed or stolen, in the accounts of previous Governments. The reputed scandal was a mare's nest; the absent documents and vouchers had been overlooked or put away. The Auditor found his

1 Newton MSS. 1, 95.   2 Ibid. 1, 98.

opportunity against Newton in a statutory clause which ran:

There shall not be issued out of the Exchequer of the said moneys, (that is, the Mint Customs duties) in any one year, for the fees and salaries of the Officers of the Mint or Mints, and towards the providing, maintaining and repairing of the houses, offices and buildings, and other necessaries for assaying, melting down and coining, above the sum of £3,000 sterling money.

So it had been prescribed in the Coinage Act of 1666, which put the cost of the Mint on taxes instead of seigniorage; that Act being septennial, the clause had since been re-enacted five times, two of them in Newton's Mastership, nor had it been otherwise altered when, in 1706, the limit was raised to £3,500. But no one knew a meaning for the phrase 'necessaries for assaying, melting down and coining'. A conclave of lawyers in James II's reign could only agree that it did not mean what it said, since that would preclude any large coinage; it must signify something, as an absurdity of Parliament was, legally, unthinkable, but each learned man favoured a different something. Mint practice was to restrain within the limit the total of salaries, of construction and repairs of buildings, and of the State's contribution to officers' meals on Board days. Harley drew into its ambit miscellaneous outlay, nominally under the Warden, 'which', Newton said, 'was never reckoned before to make part of the allowance by Parliament, as may be seen by the accounts that have been made up and declared for thirty years before'. An overspending of £99. 9s. was produced by the Auditor's unexpected classification in the 1712 accounts, from which he commanded its deletion.

Newton argued that when statutes were ambiguous old custom had the force of law; he tried to rationalise the

clause as a control on permanent expenditure, which did
not vary in proportion to the amount of coinage, and
optional outlays where extravagance was possible; and
claimed that all the expenditure of the year had been
necessary and most careful.[1] But, after much adding of
different items that all left the Mint within the limit, he
gave the Lord Treasurer's brother best, and 'to make
things easy' cut out of the accounts a bricklayer's bill for
£130, though Harley would have passed another £30. 11s.
'had we found vouchers to make it just so'.[2] Financial
years were not then so hide-bound as now; the withdrawn
item was simply inserted in the pending account as expenditure of 1713, and duly passed. But other items to a total
of £27. 7s. were disallowed in the 1713 accounts[3] for some
reason not recorded, and seemingly proved a dead loss to
the Master.

These final vexations coincided with the publication, in
June 1713, of the second edition of the *Principia*, which
Newton had been steadily amending since the Scottish
recoinage.

On 25 November 1713, just before the annual elections
in the Royal Society, one of the Fellows, John Chamberlain, wrote to put his various votes at Newton's disposal:
'I beg the favour of you to mark the enclosed list for me
between this and Monday next just as you intend to do
your own both for the new councillors and new officers,
all but one whom I desire to choose freely and whom I
would make perpetual Dictator of the Society if that
depended only on the vote of your very faithful humble
servant.'[4] This was the election at which 'Newton had like
to be left out of the Presidency',[5] but the three blank pages

1 Newton MSS. i, 334, 339.   2 Ibid. i, 86.
3 Master's Accounts.   4 Ibid. ii, 334.
5 More, p. 538.

of this delicate compliment were used by the recipient for scribbling paper. He drafted on one the Report of his Commission on Greenwich Observatory; the burden of it was that Flamsteed should be paid for the equipment with which he had provided the Observatory, subject to verification of his ownership.[1] This might serve as an example of 'a most fearful cautious and suspicious temper' of which Whiston complained.[2] It but left to paying officers their proper duty.

Another page was devoted to the annihilation of an application by Charles Tonnah and William Dale, which had hung about since 15 August. This pair had invented a new metal, possibly a variety of brass, of golden likeness, and petitioned that halfpence and farthings might be coined of it to the tune of £165,000. Newton wrote that nearly enough of these coins were already in circulation; that they ought to be made, like other money, of a substance with a known market quotation, and at as little profit on that price as would cover Mint costs, which calculation was not possible with a secret patent; that mimicry of gold was perilous to the general interest; and that the new metal seemed liable to be itself counterfeited by brass. He copied this letter with a changed word or two and dispatched it to the Treasury on 27 January 1714;[3] the draft was probably penned the same day or within a few days before.

Finally, a sketch of Newton's rejoinder to Leibnitz' claim to priority in the invention of the calculus was written over Chamberlain's letter. Leibnitz' brag, in 1705, that he had been copied by Newton attracted public retorts from two mathematicians of standing, one English, the other long resident in England, that it had been the other way round; their attacks goaded Leibnitz into two appeals to

1 Newton MSS. ii, 334.   2 More, p. 512.
3 Try.pp. CLXII, 252, printed in Shaw, Writers, p. 186.

the Royal Society for protection. On receipt of the first, Newton made an oral statement (March 1711) from the President's chair on the chronology of his fluxions. The critics of Leibnitz were counselled to temperance, but without much effect on their attitude. On the second appeal, the Society appointed a committee to scrutinise the letters and records of the pertinent period; Newton guided the committee, which was appointed on 6 March and reported on 24 April 1712, through the maze of obscure and already ancient matter, and drafted or helped to draft their report. The committee found that Newton had discovered his fluxions fifteen years before Leibnitz began to publish the differential method. Their report was published on 3 January 1713 for private circulation, under the title of *Commercium Epistolicum D. Johannis Collins et aliorum de analisi promota*.

Leibnitz answered on 29 July, with an anonymous pamphlet, the *Charta Volans* or Flying Letter, and again with another anonymous article in the *Journal Littéraire* of November–December 1713. Both included—without the name but with sufficient indication of the author—a private letter received by Leibnitz from an eminent mathematician, Bernoulli, who hitherto had accorded him priority, but now confined himself to comments on the unjudicial procedure of the committee. In the second, Leibnitz tried to buttress up his case by charging Newton with stealing other men's thunder on a number of other subjects. A little later, he sought to blacken Newton's repute otherwise by attacking his theology to members of the Royal family.

Newton then got Keill, one of his previous champions, to publish a summary of the successive old documents in the *Journal Littéraire* of July–August 1714; drafted, pretty well by Royal command, a letter to Leibnitz on the sequence of the discoveries and acknowledgements, which Leibnitz' patron, now on the Throne of England, heartily approved. In 1715 he drew up and published a summary of *Commercium Epistolicum*, and further translated this summary into Latin, to be published in 1722.

It was a part of his comments on one of his rival's moves that Newton dashed off, in early 1714, after[1] dealing with the gold-like metal, across the face of Chamberlain's letter. Other stray bits of comment, besides those written on virgin paper,[2] were drafted, some in English, some in Latin, on the blanks of reports on the worn state of the English silver circulation[3] (February 1713), on other proposals for coinage of copper,[4] and on the Mint's poor progress in coining that metal[5] (April 1714). Leibnitz seemed to be subconsciously associated with degraded forms of coin.

The sincerity and conviction of these unshapen drafts are clear. It is 'of consequence to know the times when men of note fell into their meditations'. Leibnitz is reproached for falsifying history. He is held to have put himself out of court by producing no evidence from 1705 onwards of his alleged priority of invention, and by putting about anonymous statements. He feels free to 'question the candour of other men...and insists upon his own candour, as if it were injustice to question it'. And then tries to ride off by introduction of red herrings: 'he will neither prove nor answer but betakes himself to clamour and to new disputes about Philosophy'.

The Newtonian system indeed is held in these drafts to be the more beautiful and more universal, 'as it is the oldest notation so it is the best', but the main affair of the argu-

---

1 The other material was drafted on the blank pages; the anti-Leibnitz draft had to run over the original writing.
2 Sotheby, 279.
3 Newton MSS. II, 88.
4 Ibid. II, 340, 352.
5 Ibid. II, 453.

ment is concrete dates, the day, month and year of twelve letters that passed between the parties. Newton's correspondent is asked to publish these or indicated extracts, without comment. 'Let every man consult the records and form his own judgment upon them.'[1] Leibnitz' prevarications and his charge that Newton had copied from him and built upon his work suggest, as Conduitt for instance said, that he had done precisely that with Newton. But Leibnitz was a German, and one who had been engaged in political propaganda. He was now a dependent of the German Court of Hanover; the repute of the Court and his prosperity might be advanced by advertisement of his mathematical achievements. Newton held an ancient executive post at pleasure only; the terms of his bargain would at the least need renewal on the accession of a new monarch, and that monarch was likely and proved to be Leibnitz' present protector, with a vested interest in his stock; moreover, the political opponents of the party with which Newton was associated seemed to be in power. His worldly interest was all against entering upon such a quarrel. However, Newton continued to hold his Mastership throughout the reign of George I, while Leibnitz, discredited, died on 14 November 1716, 'to be buried like a robber'.

Pepys had tried to enlist the talents of Newton, in the year that he became Warden, to discover some method of ascertaining longitude out at sea.[1] The House of Commons formed a committee twenty years later to study a State stimulus to science to meet this nautical need. Newton's old protegé, Whiston, and Ditton laid before it, not without hope of reward, a way out by firing big guns on shore. His criticism was sought on 11 June 1714; he gave the committee a list of potential methods and tepidly commended

1 Newton MSS. II, 353.

Whiston's idea, provided men used to the sea should think it practicable. This evidence was submitted in writing, as was but proper for a balanced technical report. When the paper had been read, the Chairman asked if Whiston's scheme was any good; Newton hesitated, as one does at an inquiry whether one's deliberate grey is black or white; Whiston, seeing that silence meant a black ball, called out: 'Good in part'; and Newton repeated this phrase of his evidence. Spite has inferred unreadiness of speech from his pause; it looks more like honesty in the trying air of a Select Committee. A note of the possible lines of attack and of the books of tables required was made by him on papers of 1709—whether for this committee or for personal consideration does not appear.

Parliament was so much impressed by the problem and so little impressed by Whiston that it offered a prize of £20,000 for a practical solution; one-half of this was won by John Harrison in 1726 by the construction of an accurate chronometer.[1]

1 Brewster, pp. 199, 204.

CHAPTER IX

COPPER COINAGE FOR ENGLAND

THE licence to a company to get copper struck by the Moneyers ran out in 1701; no halfpence or farthings were issued for the next sixteen years. Persons anxious to make money for themselves and small coin for England, Ireland or America, poured in petitions for new licences. The former contractors, owners of mines or of rolling mills, the garrisons who had held Derry and Enniskillen against James in 1688, the Mint Moneyers themselves, all quoted their deserts and distresses which a bit of State business would relieve. Newton progressively elaborated the standard Mint doctrines: copper coinage should be run by the Mint for Exchequer account; then, no motive of private profit could harm the quantity or quality of metal in the coins, nor swell the total coinage past the country's needs. Besides, the face value of the coin ought to be its intrinsic value, less only the cost of manufacture and distribution. Intrinsic value of copper and of gold and silver coin had thus nothing in common, except to the ear. A new guinea or shilling was meant to return a guinea's or a shilling's worth of bullion when melted down; which was in truth irrational, as melting them down was criminal; but a shilling's worth of halfpence could in any case contain only sixpence or sevenpence worth of metal. Newton was to wrestle long and vainly for the odd penny. Howbeit, the false analogy held the field, and, when petitioners offered the Government a profit of 2d. on each pound weight of coin made, he could dispose of the bait with the questions, Why not 8d.? Why not 14d.?

Our present pence are the size of those halfpence, but if the weights were again halved, no theorist would worry about intrinsic value.

Newton is said to have been offered £6,000 to put one of these coinage proposals through; but no official or even Minister could possibly have got away with such a bribe in connection with coinage; conditions in the public service had greatly changed in the generation since Pepys.

The Master had been ready to strike additional copper coin for the American Plantations in 1703, of an 'intrinsic value' adjusted to take account of local prices of copper, shipping costs and a profit for the local governments, and adopted a private business man's idea that the mainland and West Indies should be divided roughly into four currency areas and different coins made for each (p. 48). But nothing came of it.

England, he contended and the Treasury agreed, was already amply supplied with coppers. Parliament had imposed a year's holiday during the private issue of 1694–1701 on account of gluts of coin, and he still heard of such gluts, for example from the Post Office. He estimated the necessary circulation at the outside at £120,000 to £130,000, the amount of that private issue, and its annual depletion by wastage at £2,500 to £3,000. Even in 1713, after twelve years' cessation of coinage, with Scotland added, with counterfeiting of coppers, which the Mint commonly regarded as a symptom of shortage, prevalent and with shortages in London, he maintained that the surviving coins were enough. But that autumn, the insidious Harley, Earl of Oxford, in a personal interview decided that a new coinage should start. Newton, of course, wanted his coins to be at least up to the last State issue; the private issue in between had been a little lower in weight, at 42 halfpence to the pound avoirdupois, and in fineness of copper, and atrociously executed. He estimated that it could be done and the initial costs of new equipment covered, if the Mint, in place of buying blanks, purchased copper in ingots and cast, rolled and cut its own. For precision, he looked round for a definition of good copper. No method for its analysis was known, but inquiry of the trade produced a practical test. A lump of copper, when heated and beaten thin with a sledge, might either break up, or crack round the edges, or retain its coherence; the several results were signs of increasing degrees of purity, and corresponded to different price levels. Newton noted the temperature to which the metal should be raised first as dark red, then as the melting-point of standard silver, finally as a red heat. Copper which would not crack under the hammer test when heated to redness accordingly became the specification for coinage copper, and so continued till the middle of the nineteenth century. He also decided to use the cheapest copper which would pass the test, as the extra price of the finest marks would reduce the size of the coins, to the temptation of counterfeiters, while the greater fineness of the coins could not be demonstrated.

Up to the last moment, he had taken for granted the addition of a little tin, under $\frac{1}{4}$ per cent, to ease minting, but now forbade any such adulteration, as a detraction from intrinsic value.

Experimental minting of 'a few tons' began in the autumn of 1713. It was found that if the copper was cast thin enough, the castings were bad, while the horse-drawn mills of the Mint had not the power to reduce thick fillets to coin thickness. A new type of furnace was built and seemed to overcome the difficulty. Next spring, Newton produced presentable coins for the inspection of the Lord Treasurer. The Treasury called in a copper magnate, James Bertie; he declared that Newton's coins were coarse copper;

that their beautiful burnish was artificial and would not last; and that he could make pure copper coins more cheaply.[1] Newton tested the coins and found that they would indeed not stand the hammer, but cracked; he could only suppose that in spite of orders and of his personal supervision, the zeal of the Melter had added a little tin.[2]

In the autumn of 1714 Newton reported that to start with ingots was beyond the Mint, and that he had obtained tenders for supply of ready-made fillets of coin thickness, of which he advised the acceptance of the best. This put the distribution of the resulting coin on the copper merchant, who wanted nearly three halfpence a pound weight for the service, but would, Newton thought, come down to a penny.[3] If so, no more than 40 halfpence need be struck to the pound. But Lord Oxford had fallen in July; indeed, a few months later, he was imprisoned in the Comptroller's house in the Mint (p. 103). The new Treasury Lords may have lost interest; at any rate they boggled at the proposed provision of a penny for cost of distribution of coin, and all question of copper coinage fell into abeyance for three years. Queen Anne's farthings, at one time priced above rubies by common report, and her double-headed halfpence, were but strays from these experiments. No copper coin was issued in England under Anne.

By April 1717 the scarcity of coppers was apparently causing acute inconvenience. In that month, too, there was a change of Government. On the 30th, an advertisement in the *Gazette* invited competitive tenders for the supply of rolled copper fillets, no longer raw metal, to the Mint. Responses reached the Treasury during May; they were forwarded in July to Newton for his analysis and

---

1 Newton MSS. II, 325, 414.   2 Ibid. II, 211.
3 Ibid. II, 308, 363.

recommendation.[1] Meantime he had advised that department that the total copper coinage should be £28,000 to £37,000, but that not more than 30 or 40 tons—£5,500 to £7,400—should be struck in a year lest his consumption should affect the price of copper; and that, though this had risen twopence a pound in the last two years, the coins could still be struck at the old rate of 40 halfpence to the pound.[2] But when he came to select the best offer, which he did on 3 August after a conference with the tenderers, the price of fillets proved to have increased more than raw metal, by fourpence a pound in all, and the Moneyers, realising that a higher standard of work would be required than at the turn of the century, had also raised their charge. He had to recommend coins that ran no more than 46 halfpence to the pound.[3] This was agreed; a contract for the supply of fillets ready to be cut into blanks was accepted by him on 27 August;[4] a Royal Warrant was issued to him on 13 September to authorise this step and the subsequent coinage,[5] while the Exchequer advanced him £500 to finance its start.[6]

The primary coining tools were still being cut at the end of November, when Newton again insisted that further experimentation was necessary to settle the details of mass coinage, as it 'was different from that of coarse copper and more difficult and not yet practised in England'.[7] On account of 'the importunity of the public', coinage started in January 1718,[8] with dies dated the previous year, without this respite; considerable changes in technique were later found to be required; thus, annealing and cleaning were transferred from the fillet to the blank stage, and

1 Newton MSS. II, 366.   2 Ibid. II, 346, 356.
3 Ibid. II, 443.   4 Ibid. II, 319.
5 Ibid. II, 425.   6 Master's Accounts.
7 Newton MSS. II, 245.   8 Try.pp. CCLIII, 28.

from the contractor to the Moneyers, who raised their charges again by three farthings a pound. Newton for a while paid a half farthing of this himself; the bulk and finally the whole of the increased fee was borne by the contractor.[1] Seeing that copper coinage by the Mint had started more than forty years before, its resumption was a strange series of miscalculations.

The unsuccessful tenderers also made trouble. They had first tried to form a ring and get the favoured competitor to raise his price. Then, they alleged favouritism in allotting contracts, scandalous conduct in the Mint Master and poor quality in his coins. By way of appeal to the Commons, persons were set at the door of the House to hand out anonymous pamphlets with these charges. On the last point, Newton insisted that metal must be examined by prescribed physical tests and not by the eye; he urged also that coining methods were in process of change; on the first, he could show that a good many of the rejected offers were higher; those which were cheaper were unreliable.[2] On subsequent complaints of defective coins, he pointed out that 'amongst the moneys newly coined there will always be some pieces faulty in form. It always was and always will be so in the coinage of gold and silver and the coinage of fine copper is more difficult...and I have caused half a ton of such copper to be melted down again.'[3] At the end of the coinage, the Mint Board had to fine the Moneyers for issuing copper coin which the Board had condemned as light. The Corporation had simply taken it back and mixed it with heavier coin to produce a satisfactory average weight. The Treasury had decided that no provision should be made for the wide distribution of the new coins; those who wanted a supply came or sent to

1 Newton MSS. ii, 428, 429, 455.   2 Ibid. ii, 452.
3 Ibid. ii, 455.

the Mint for their needs. It is unlikely that circulation far from London was rapid. Early in 1719, when some £6,000 had been coined, the Treasury suspended operations, though Newton thought that there was still an unsatisfied public demand.[1] The coinage was presently resumed; when its full term of seven years was completed and it stopped in January 1725, £30,288. 17s. 2d. had been issued.[2]

1 Newton MSS. II, 448.   2 Try.pp. CCLIII, 28.

CHAPTER X

UNDER GEORGE I

THE fears that the good Queen Anne might be succeeded by her brother, a Roman Catholic, were set
at rest by the accession of George I. We have seen
how his Protestant creed coloured Newton's ideas for the
Coronation Medal and altered the King's title on the coins
(p. 56). Newton sought to serve the cause further; he
drafted an Act for introduction into Parliament, which
recited the pretensions of the Church of Rome, and would
have enforced a declaration by all and sundry in a Court of
Law of individual belief that the said Church 'is in doctrine
and worship a false uncharitable and idolatrous church',
while Lutheran and Calvinist churches across the sea did
not imperil the Church of England.[1]

In November 1714 his interest in education was again
manifested by the preparation of a syllabus for Mr Stone's
School.[2]

It may be that prosecution of counterfeiters languished
under Warden Peyton; the post of prosecuting clerk
dropped during 1714, and complaints were made of
Peyton's slackness, which the Mint hotly repudiated.[3] Sir
Richard Sandford, who succeeded him at the end of 1714,
went direct to the Treasury for the revival of the clerkship.
The request was referred back to Newton. He, in backing
the proposal, framed in supplement of the salary a schedule
of fees, nominally for expenses, for each item of business
in town or country, in place of the haphazard control by

---

1 Brewster, II, 280. 2 Newton MSS. II, 337.
3 M.R. 8, 108; Newton MSS. I, 450.

the Treasury of the fund created in 1706. Whether by virtue of this improvement or luck in the choice of Courtney Pinckney, no doubt one of the clan of that name who held a lot of servile Court appointments in Somerset House, the post in the new hands swelled forthwith into that of Solicitor to the Mint. The Warden became a gentleman of complete leisure; not only was he relieved of work only fit for an Attorney, but questions beyond the Solicitor seem to have been diverted to the Master.

Within the Warden's sphere was certainly a matter raised by the arrest and committal to the Tower in 1715 of the Lord Treasurer, Oxford. The Lieutenant put the prisoner in the house of the Comptroller, and set a guard about it. It was Newton who composed and signed a protest to the new Board of Treasury against this involuntary trespass in the Mint by his late Chief:

My Lords, the safety of the coinage depends upon keeping the Mint out of the hands of the Garrison, and the safety of prisoners depends upon keeping them in a legal custody under the jurisdiction of their keepers. And I am humbly of opinion not only that the prisoner be removed into a legal custody, but that something be done which may hinder the invasion of the Mint from being drawn into a precedent.[1]

In March or April 1716 two Scotsmen brought to the Lord Mayor of London samples of ore from two veins of silver which had been discovered by Sir John Erskine on his property near Stirling and worked by him from June 1715 to February 1716. Sir John's absence for a couple of months during this period on the Jacobite rebellion of 1715 did not stay the operations, but when they were abandoned and the diggings filled in, two of the discharged Scots came

1 Newton MSS. III, 407.

south to give information. The brother of Sir John's wife thought it prudent to let the Palace know, about the same time that the Lord Mayor was approached.[1] The samples were sent to Newton, who confirmed the richness of the ore, but added cautiously, 'where it grows does not yet appear to me'.[2] He was asked to have a look at the mine, but 'represented himself unacquainted with such matters', and suggested that the King might bring an expert from his German mines.[3] A Justus Brandshagen, by profession a physician, was fetched accordingly, and sent north with the two informers as assistants. From London to Edinburgh, 'was three weeks and two days in a dangerous voyage, and in two storms we lost two masts and were thrice driven on the Sand-banckes. When the ship was repairing, all the passengers went ashore which was very chargeable to me.'[4] Newton was responsible for all general instructions: what areas to explore, what size samples to take; how to witness the sealing up of samples. He was also paymaster and accountant for the expedition, and kept it so short of funds that work had to wait, or at least waited, till the good German 'was so happy as to borrow £66' in Edinburgh. The party spent four months in Scotland and another three in London on writing their report—all far too leisurely in Newton's opinion, as they were paid by the day. He had cleared the accounts by the summer of 1717,[5] but seven years later, in 1724, a lawsuit was launched against him by one of the Scots for £62. 10s.[6] and another claim came from Edinburgh for £10 that Brandshagen had borrowed.[7]

After the Peace of Ryswick the golden stream from

---

1 Newton MSS. III, 246.   2 Ibid. III, 268.
3 Ibid. III, 246.   4 Ibid. III, 266.
5 Ibid. III, 264.   6 Ibid. III, 240.
7 Ibid. III, 243.

Portugal was swollen by another from France, our late
enemies burning to invest in British Government securi-
ties.[1] In 1713 the Mint coined £600,000 odd; in 1714,
£1,380,000; in 1715, £1,826,000. The fees of Master,
Melter and Moneyers rose correspondingly, but the public
fund of the Mint was emptied of the savings accumulated
during the lean years. Its annual income from the Customs
duties averaged £9,600 in this triennium: its expenditure
was half as much again at £14,380. By February 1716
there remained in the bottom of the chest only enough for
one more month's coinage.[2] The Coinage Act being due
for its periodical renewal, Newton asked for a 50 per cent
increase in the Customs duties; but far from scrapping the
otiose divisional limits on different classes of outlay, which
had brought him into conflict with the Audit Office, he
wrought for their extension to Edinburgh, that the two
places might be alike.[3] On both points he was overruled.
Simplification was done for him; the Act of 1716 ran all
the limits into a single figure of £15,000 a year for both
Mints together. The Customs were not altered, but the
Treasury was authorised, if need be, to apply other funds
to the support of the Mints. In September of the year
following, Newton had to remonstrate with the Treasury
for handing over to Edinburgh the £1,200 of coinage
monies available, when the London Mint had but £310
left to defray the current quarter's expenditure of £1,700,
and to press for a grant from those other sources, 'the
Melter and Moneyers being out of pocket and the clerks
not able to subsist without their salaries'.[4] That was the
worst moment. The coinage expenditure of 1715 had been
£19,557, but from 1717 to Newton's death it only averaged
£8,708 a year, so that the Mint acquired once more the

1 Newton MSS. II, 124.   2 Ibid. I, 325.
3 Ibid. III, 57.   4 Ibid. I, 372.

comfortable balance of £22,278.[1] The decision against change of taxation had justified itself in a very short time.

The expansion of gold emphasised the paucity of silver coin. Silver was imported in even larger bulk than it was exported: 'immense quantities were wrought into plate';[2] but none came to be coined, except the trifling by-product of native lead mines, whose owners believed themselves obliged by their charters to tender it to the Mint. At the same time, the existing silver circulation had shrunk away by the abstraction of all unworn coin to be melted down. The contrast between the two sorts of bullion was such that the closure of the Mint to gold coinage was considered.[3]

In April 1717 the Government was dismissed. Lord Stanhope took over the Treasury. Someone remembered that Newton had twice pressed them to reduce the value put upon the guinea. In the ordinary course, the probable outcome would have been discussed with him before the Treasury, on 12 August, instructed him to report on the ratio of the values of gold and silver, and on the best way to halt the melting down of silver coin. Newton's first reaction, as shown by drafts of the famous report of 21 September 1717, was that currency habits had changed, and in a respect that we should think vital. Whereas England had in 1702 measured prices in silver, 'gold is now become our standard money and silver is a commodity which rises and falls here in its price as it does in Spain'.[4] This judgement was endorsed by Conduitt in 1730: 'nine parts in ten or more of all payments in England are now made in gold'; and 'the greatest part of the silver now remaining in the nation and most likely to remain is in sixpences and shillings', which were much worn.[5]

1 Master's Accounts.   2 Conduitt, p. 12.
3 Newton MSS. II, 124.   4 Ibid. II, 108.
5 Conduitt, p. 15.

Since Newton was clear that the standard of value could be one metal only, he began to propose, as so often had been proposed and was to be proposed again, that the weights of silver coins should be so reduced that a pound troy made 64s. 6d. instead of 62s.[1] He had observed that silver coin when a little worn was saved for circulation by its inferior weight.[2] But this solution would not have suited his masters; in the final form, he omitted his observations and translated the conclusion into the mathematically equivalent but impracticable proposition that silver coin should retain its weight and be left to rise in value by force of scarcity. 'If things be left alone till silver money be a little scarcer, the gold will fall of itself. For people are already backward to give silver for gold, and will in a little time refuse to make payments in silver without a premium, as they do in Spain, and this premium will be an abatement in the value of the gold.' This paragraph was tucked away near the end of the report, and was presumably not meant as a recommendation, but to warn off those who wanted the guinea left alone.

The last paragraph of the report dismissed the idea of temporary alleviation of scarcity by coining plate, as in 1709 and 1711; the silver was safe in the expensive form of plate, and if coined would certainly be exported.

The foundation of the main argument was the two tables of continental coins of 1702, amended in spots and multiplied by the researches of a decade and a half. As before, values were calculated to two places of decimals. The new issue of France was there, but so was the abandoned one; most of the coins were old; some of the German had been issued before the Thirty Years War. The report showed indeed how much more silver a weight of gold would buy

1 Newton MSS. II, 124.   2 Ibid. II, 69.

in England than in various parts of West Europe, except
Spain and Portugal. It equally though obscurely said: a
small difference in valuation controls the movement of
coin; a reduction of the guinea by 8d. or 1s. would bring
England into line with the Continent; a reduction of 6d.
will not; nothing will stop the drain to the East, where
silver is esteemed much more dearly and gold much more
cheaply than in England. Newton may have been making
out a case by special pleading, either to meet official wishes
or for the sake of his own consistency, for these points
were put so agreeably and in such nice proportions that
the reader is convinced that 6d. off, which was probably
the only figure politically practicable, was a moderate and
statesmanlike measure. 'But if only 6d. were taken off at
present, it would diminish the temptation to export
and melt down the silver coin, and by the effects
would show hereafter better than can appear at present
what further reduction would be most convenient to the
public.'[1]

The Government's decision was taken on Saturday,
21 December; Newton was bidden that evening draw up a
schedule of reductions for other gold coins; it was ready
next day—figures proportionate to sixpence off the guinea
series, and a flat sixpence off the old, and badly worn, coins
that were valued at 23s. 6d. And the Proclamation came
out on that Sunday.[2]

Newton's report, simultaneously released to the Press,
seems to have carried conviction. But 'blinding with
science' could not prevent some disadvantages. The Mint
itself dropped £11 on its small holding in guineas; other
Government departments lost more; private and com-

---

1 Try.pp. CCVIII, 43. The report is printed in Shaw, Writers,
pp. 188 ff.
2 Newton MSS. II, 117, 120.

mercial owners of gold coin who had no recourse against the Exchequer showed a resentment which had not appeared in the late 1690's, when gold was a 'commodity', and which killed any idea of a further reduction.

Besides this, there was a large export of gold to Holland,[1] a rise to £4. 0s. 6d. of the home price of gold, and some disturbance of the exchanges. Newton, set on his defence, held that these manifestations were due to other causes, had in part preceded the change, and had already (20 October 1718) ceased.[2] The sole effect of the reduction of the guinea was that England got her new gold 6d. an ounce cheaper; to undo it would 'revive the corrupt trade of exporting silver to buy gold abroad and importing gold to buy silver at home'. Conduitt, twelve years later, summed up the absence of results: 'the reduction of 6d. upon the guinea had no lasting effect upon the exchange; did not apparently lower the price of silver; nor bring an ounce of silver to the Mint'.[3]

As another cure for the silver crisis, a Bill to allow the export of English coin and prevent that of bullion, on the lines worked out by Newton in 1701, was considered, but thought useless.[3] A quarter guinea was also issued in 1718 to make good the shortage of five shilling pieces; it proved popular as a curiosity, but was too tiny for use as a coin. Only 37,380 were struck, and the experiment was dropped. All effort to maintain a silver currency was abandoned for the rest of the century.

It was apparently in the latter part of 1717 that, at the request of the Princess of Wales, Newton drew up for her personal perusal, and on the condition that it should not be communicated to others, his *Short Chronicle from the first things in Europe to the Conquest of Persia by Alexander the*

1 Newton MSS. II, 119.   2 Ibid. II, 124.
3 Conduitt, p. 18.

Great. At any rate papers of that period were used for jotting down of notes.[1]

Newton's theological works seem generally not to have been dated; at or soon after this date, he was engaged on one which dealt with the bond between a church and its members, the obligations assumed on baptism, the right of excommunication under temporal by-laws, and the various uses of the word 'God' in the Scriptures.[2] It was probably a little earlier that he was engaged on an erudite account of recondite heresies of the first three centuries.[3]

1 Newton MSS. II, 236, 409.   2 Ibid. v, 33, 39.
3 Ibid. v, 37, 38.

CHAPTER XI

CLOSING YEARS

THE year 1720 opened with a fresh attempt of the Tower to enlarge its grip on one of the buildings in the Mint, the Master Smith's house, to provide clerical accommodation and additional barracks. Newton asked for delay and a considered review to prevent disputes, keep the coinage safe, and secure space for more coining presses hereafter. Meantime, he demanded that no soldiers should be lodged within the Mint gates. In the memorandum and five drafts of his letter, he detailed the history of the disputed house back to 1553.[1]

Some unusual bits of business then came along. Great Britain, having agreed by Treaty to pay Sweden 288,000 Imperial dollars, the Treasury on 5 April 1726 asked Newton what an Imperial dollar might be. Equally puzzled, he inclined at first to hold that it was no coin at all, but an abstraction like the pound sterling; if so, it was best represented by 'the Common Dollar of Germany', which was 3s. 6d. English and made the debt £50,400.[2] But on revising his draft next morning, he substituted: 'I am told that the Imperial Dollar is sometimes taken for the Common Dollar but more usually for the Rix Dollar, and that the word Reichs or Rycks Thaler signifies Imperial Dollar. But I am not skilled in the German language.' He went on that the rix dollars of the different German States varied in their value from 4s. 2d. to 4s. 8d. English, but that books of exchange gave the value as 4s. 6d. and he

---

1 Newton MSS. III, 400, 425, 426, 427, 433, 439.
2 Ibid. II, 180.

accordingly raised the sum due to £64,800.[1] The Treasury gave the Swedes £72,000.

The Navy paid its crews off in paper tickets to be encashed at a Navy Office—after inordinate delays, when the Exchequer was low. To check the frauds that were worked with these tickets, a Mr Orlebar devised a pay token, part brass, part copper. The invention was referred to Newton; he was able to commend it for greater safety against forgery[2] (16 May 1720).

Everyone has heard of the South Sea Bubble of 1720. On 27 July, at the top peak of the boom, when the Bubble was at point to burst, Newton, who had previously ventilated cold distrust of the gambling fever, instructed Fauquiere to invest £650 a year of his annuities in a new issue of South Sea stock. Catherine Conduitt afterwards lamented that her uncle had lost £20,000 by this act. The purchase would invite a more acid criticism if it had been inspired by belief in a rising market; just four days earlier, on 23 June, Newton had sold £200 per annum of South Sea Company annuities on behalf of the estate of Thomas Hall, his old guarantor, of which he was a trustee.[3]

But de Villamil has shown that the transaction was merely a transfer from one South Sea stock to another of similar standing, and that the 'loss' of £20,000 was the profit which might have been taken on the original investment by selling out at the top of the market.[4] Catherine was a hard woman.

An inventor, John Rotherham, pressed on the Mint in August 1720 a discovery which would make the coins more durable, defeat men who abstracted a little bullion with acids, and prevent all counterfeiting, 'whereby the lives of many persons in time to come will be saved'. Moreover,

1 Try.pp. CCXVII, 31. 2 Sotheby, 170.
3 Ibid. 300 (1). 4 de Villamil, pp. 19–27.

the new method, while saving the Government up to
£20,000 a year, would swell the Master's and other salaries
in the Mint. As reward for all this, he sought no more
than a post in the Mint at £1,000 a year for himself and
his heirs for ever.[1] When the Master was not attracted,
Rotherham tried the Lords Justices,[2] whom Newton could
only advise: 'he offers nothing to be examined and without
examination I am in the dark and know not what report to
make. I take him to be a trifler, more fit to embroil the
coinage than to amend it.' The trifler, after a year's medi-
tation, placed still grander prospects before the Privy
Council; Newton thought that the time had come to see
the inventor; and the octogenarian with a quarter of a century of public service behind him armed himself for the
interview by drawing up a catechism of twelve questions.[3]

When Rotherham petitioned the King, six years later,
to make the Mint buy his secret, his visions had grown
phantasmal and his lunacy palpable.[4]

The Warden, now William Thomson, had evidently
shifted his last few duties on the Master. On 1 March
1721 it was Newton who refused a reward to an informer
who had reported certain presses as capable of being used
for coinage, on the grounds that the proceedings taken had
in the main failed, that there was no precedent for a reward
where a conviction was not obtained, and that a new
precedent would be dangerous.[5]

About the middle of 1722, on recovery from a long illness, Newton put in hand the preparation of a third and
revised edition of the *Principia*. Printing began in December 1723 or January 1724, and the considerable labour of
amendment on proof sheets went on, in correspondence

1 Newton MSS. 1, 492.   2 Ibid. 1, 486.
3 Ibid. 1, 448, 489, 490, 494.   4 Try.pp. CCLXV, 20.
5 Newton MSS. 1, 464.

with the editor, Pemberton, during the next two years. The book was issued in February or March 1726.[1]

As long ago as 1698, Newton had supported a claim by the eight Mint clerks for the increase by a half of the salaries granted them in 1662. The highest paid group got £40, the lowest £10 a year. The heavy clerical labour on the Great Recoinage and in straightening accounts afterwards left no spare time for other employment; Newton observed besides that the salaries when fixed 'might be a better maintenance than £60 p.a. would be now'.[2] The request was turned down by the Treasury, and further proposals in 1702, 1705 and 1718 had no more success, but in August 1722 Newton at last secured a rise of a quarter for this staff.[3] Two years later a repercussion had to be admitted on the salary of the Porter, who was a pluralist and well to do, and for the Assayer's Fireman, in whose view £25 a year 'was not a maintenance for a single person', especially one 'who was exposed to great danger and hazard in his health and life' by his duties.[4]

The coppers supplied by the Mint were meant for Great Britain, but in Ireland, workmen and small traders had to make do with a hotch-potch of imitation coins, manufactured without control or limit by any Tom, Dick or Harry. Representations about hardships and frauds practised on the poor were made to London, where, after examination of offers by his competitors, William Wood, a frequent tenderer of copper to the Mint, was licensed in 1722 to make halfpence and farthings for the sister Isle. About the same time he secured a contract to produce coin for America, of which the result was the handsome Rosa Americana series. The Irish coin began to be issued in 1723. The political and official classes in the Island went hay-

---

1 Brewster, II, 304–7.   2 Newton MSS. II, 474.
3 Ibid. I, 26.   4 Ibid. I, 92.

wire. Of menace to profits on substitute coinages no one spoke, but patriots raged with suitable invective on the absence of consultation with the Dublin Parliament; on the corruption and looseness of the contract; on the badness and excessive quantity of the coinage. The constitutional point was unsound; neither in Ireland nor in England had Parliament been approached on any previous copper coinage, not even on the English issue started in 1718. Wood's licence was hedged about with such safeguards against abuse as had never been heard of before; judging by the costs of the Tower Mint, and its estimates of the expence of distribution of coin in England, his profits, if the contract had run its full course, could hardly have exceeded $7\frac{1}{2}$ per cent on his outlay, and any bribe to the King's mistress came out of that modest return; Wood indeed offered to sell the coins to the Irish Government at only 1d. a pound over the Mint's cost of production of English coppers. The coins were heavier and intrinsically more valuable than any issued before in Ireland. They were of the same finer copper as had been adopted in the English Mint, and contemporaries considered them more handsomely struck. Only the ultimate total of £100,800 Irish, that is about £93,000 English, spread over fourteen years, might be thought high for Ireland, if English needs were correctly estimated at £120,000; but the issues for five or six years at least must have been required; as for longer views, the coins were not legal tender and no one was bound to accept them.

The Privy Council in London thought well to learn the reason for all this heat, and set up a formal inquiry (April 1724), during which they suspended the coinage. To their surprise, the Dublin Parliament and the other agitators refused to give any evidence or information; fear of their fellows, they said, sealed their lips.[1]

1 Report of Committee of Privy Council, 24 July 1724.

At this late stage, Dean Swift snatched at applause with two topical sermons and the *Drapier Letters*. Gossip he set down as gospel, with figments of his own, in tune with Dublin's mood, and so fashioned the legend of Wood's corrupt coinage. He was flogging a horse that had bolted. The English Government had no inclination to do unpopular good by force; on 6 August they cut down, at Wood's own suggestion, the ultimate total to £40,000;[1] when this did not prove acceptable, they made the suspension of the copper coinage permanent. There had been issued £15,481 Irish in halfpence, and £1,086 of farthings.[2]

Newton's part in the controversy was purely technical. He drafted the specifications and safeguards against abuse in the original contract. A little later (January 1723), on the motion of the Moneyers, he asked that the Mint should coin Wood's blanks for him, partly to give the Moneyers work, partly to prevent diffusion of coining skill.[3] But this request was refused. The supervision of the quality and quantity of the coinage throughout was in his hands and was performed by an inspector, Matthew Barton, appointed by him. And he was one of the trio who finally judged the quality of the coinage by its Pyx of sample coins from each batch (27 April 1724).[4]

Newton's vigour was now definitely failing. He obtained relief in the Presidency of the Royal Society by the appointment in 1722 of a Deputy President, Martin ffoulkes, In 1725 he is said by Brewster,[5] in 1722 by More,[6] to have considered resignation from the Mint, and to have been induced to carry on by the proffer of Conduitt's help. Of Conduitt's assistance within the Mint there is no trace, but the Deputy Master, Fauquiere, took over a share of the

1 M.R. i, 213; Newton MSS. ii, 467; Try.pp. CCXLVIII, 13.
2 Newton MSS. ii, 472.   3 Ibid. ii, 464.
4 Ibid. ii, 467.   5 Brewster, ii, 130.   6 More, p. 659.

Master's duties from about 1716 onwards. He it was who managed at least the later stages of the copper coinage, and the final account was rendered and signed by him on 28 July 1725.[1] Howbeit, by that time Fauquiere was ill with dropsy, and he died on 22 September 1726.

In August 1724 the aged Master was again consulted by the First Lord on Warden's business—the question whether mercy should be shown a condemned counterfeiter; Newton's advice was firm: 'I know nothing of Edmund Metcalfe convicted at Derby Assizes of counterfeiting the coin...but...it's better to let him suffer...for these people very seldom leave off. And it's difficult to detect them.'[2]

In January 1725 Newton moved to rural Kensington for the sake of his health and the brisker air; Pitt's Buildings off Church Street were his home for his few remaining years. In November he did one curious thing. Traders' tokens had flourished in the past and had been declared illegal; their second flowering was still to come. Newton, moreover, had, after some hesitation, thought it improper in 1708 to comply officially with a request for a renewal of the Isle of Man coinage by the Earl of Derby, Lord of the Island, because 'no other money than her Majesty's should be coined in Her Majesty's Mint'; he was willing that the Moneyers might undertake it as private business,[3] but the Treasury apparently vetoed this and the coins were struck outside the Mint. Now, Newton issued orders for the Mint to make substitutes for coin for use in Curwen's coal mines at Workington: 'Let tokens be made of the form drawn above for Mr Curwen. Is. Newton.'[4]

1 Try.pp. CCLIII, 28; Shaw, Writers, pp. 199–202.
2 More, p. 453.   3 Newton MSS. II, 456, 457.
4 B.M. Add. MS. 18757, fol. 19v. cited by *Numismatic Chronicle*, 1921, p. 153.

In May 1725 Newton asserted with habitual precision and detail his title as an owner of land at his old birthplace to a share in the commons rights of Woolsthorpe.[1]

In November he made his valuation for Ireland of a new issue of Portuguese coin (p. 85). It was in November also that he received a copy of a translation of his *Short Chronicle* (p. 109), issued by a piratical French publisher with comments, though he had withheld the original English version from publication. Newton sat down to rewrite the original work, which the faithful Conduitt published after his death.[2]

Only six months (September 1726) before his death the King's Assaymaster, now his old admirer Hopton Haynes, could beg the Master to call at the Mint for personal examination of some gold ingots which were believed to be impure, though no fault could be detected by assay.[3] So long a journey was by now an undertaking; to preside over the Royal Society in early March 1727, he came up to London two days before and stayed for two days beyond the meeting. On 4 March he returned to Kensington, where he died on the 20th.

1 More, p. 664.   2 Ibid. pp. 612, 662.
3 Newton MSS. 1, 108.

CHAPTER XII

SURVEY

Newton's mathematical and scientific pursuits continued during his employment at the Mint. The combined labour did not prevent a barren reconstruction of world history, nor fresh research in theology.

In his office, concrete problems were handled with reasonable competence, in so far as no revision of accepted principle or unusual prescience was needed. The novel business of tin sales seems to have been well organised and to have run smoothly, within the limits permitted by party considerations; the recoinage at Edinburgh likewise, after the lapse of seven months from the start of planning, and after Newton had been forced temporarily off the theory of identical processes. In general the questions that arose year by year in the Mint, or which were referred to him for advice, were settled with gumption.

He had the tact to allow for political or human aspects of the larger questions, though he might not assess their exact force. It was his habit also to resort to personal interview and oral discussion on any matters of dissension. Contractors, candidates for employment, inventors and other rapscallions, were all seen in this way, and much of the correspondence with the Treasury began with or was clarified by conversations with successive Lord Treasurers, or First Lords after the office was put in commission.

Newton appears to have been a good judge and handler of men, and he had some magnetism which in many engendered an extraordinary regard and respect. Not an effusively affectionate man himself, he was a target for such affection from others.

But with all his faith in direct contacts in cases of dispute, as a good bureaucrat, he insisted on the preservation of clear and exact records, though he did not keep final copies of his own letters to the Treasury, and was zealous for the sanctity of precedent, though it were musty with years. A hundred years were to him no more than one day. Bureaucratic also was his care and restraint in considering new outlays of public money, with indifference to waste or extravagance that had become customary. The post of Warden, for instance, became a mere sinecure in his later years and could well have been scrapped a century before it was.

The enduring changes made in the Mint by Newton were only two: first, coins were required to be struck at their individual right weights; the principle of complete conformity with standard of fineness being on the contrary rejected, though a step was taken towards it; and secondly, a legal officer was introduced for legal work.

The working of the intricate constitution of the Mint was shattered by the Revolution. Transfer of supreme authority from monarch to transient ministers begot in turn the concentration of executive responsibility in more permanent heads of departments. Like Lowndes, the contemporary (1696–1724) Secretary of the Treasury, who, however, though he stayed in office for six years without a seat, was a Member of the House of Commons far longer, Newton was in effect a permanent civil servant. The contacts between the two men seem to have run almost entirely through their common minister; Newton only once mentions his colleague except as a signer of official letters. All the affairs of a department naturally tended to focus in the permanent head, and the process should have been stimulated in the Mint by the brief lives of competitive authorities; Newton saw five Wardens and four Comptrollers enter on office. But he made no attempt to codify and fix this unity in administration. On the contrary, it was under his sway that the Moneyers set up their Imperium in Imperio, treated with the Master as autonomous equals and refused work except on their own terms. After his time, the Mint organisation reverted gradually to an internal balance of powers, even though the Mastership became a ministerial office, to be enjoyed as a high step in a political career.

The currency also had suffered an upheaval, but no adjustment of Mint policy or theory was made to suit this new world. The American Plantations were left to manage with foreign coins and badly backed paper, in one even down to notes for a penny; Ireland, by its own fault no doubt, continued to rely on such English and foreign coin as the chances of trade might import; while the home country, for any transactions below a half-guinea, had to make do with a shrinking silver circulation which it was impossible to expand or even renew, and copper coin based on a theory so insufficient that control by the Mint was presently washed away by private traders' tokens. Newton neither jettisoned nor reconciled accepted coinage doctrines, but repeated the shibboleths appropriate to each kind of coin—one test of intrinsic value for copper coin, and another for gold and silver, with a third, this perhaps his own, for paper. There was some point in stripping copper coinage of profit when an arbitrary monarch had need of funds not voted by Parliament. There had been point, albeit debatable, in maintenance of the quantity of silver in coin, while silver coin was the standard; it had gone when only worn coin could circulate. Newton, recognising gold as the effective coin of the realm, did not even take steps, as had been done under Elizabeth and James I, to withdraw or penalise gold coin which had fallen excessively below its par value. As early as 1730, this neglect had resulted in critically widespread lightness among the gold currency; the hand-struck coin of 1603 to 1662, despite the lessons of the hand-struck silver, was not withdrawn till 1733.

Chemist, even alchemist, though he had been, Newton at the Mint did not rank metallurgy a science, but only a rather dull credit. 'Refining and assaying', he said, 'are manual trades';[1] and again: 'The assaymaster acts only as a manual artificer.'[2] He spoke with knowledge, for as Warden he mastered the art of assaying. His notes suggest that the technique of gold and silver assaying was novel to him at his appointment, but his manual dexterity was so phenomenal that in little over a year he could measure the difference of fineness of silver in the Scottish coins with absolute accuracy. A number of foreign coins were also assayed by him; the bulk of the work used in his reports of 1702 and 1717 was entrusted to others. Assaying of bullion received by or of coin for issue from the Mint was, of course, done by the Crown Assayer.

Newton was averse from all novelties. Coal, that warmed the domestic hearths of the Mint, was in use for smelting of copper; Wood, the Irish coiner, was experimenting with its extension to iron smelting; but though coal was successfully established in the melting house at Edinburgh, no exploration of its possibilities or limits was mooted in the London Mint. The evolution of a new type of furnace for tin called forth only directions to avoid frauds in distant experiments; a trial on Mint premises was at once vetoed. A meaningless theory obstructed the use of a little tin as alloy in copper coinage, while a more accurate measure-

1 Newton MSS. 1, 98. 2 Ibid. 1, 90.

To the Rt Honble the Earl of Oxford and
Earl Mortimer, Lord H. Treasurer of great
Britain.

May it please your Lordp

The Smith of the Mint being my servant by the
ancient constitution of the Mint, & being paid by me after
the rate of one penny per pound weight of gold coined &
one farthing ꝑ pound weight of silver coined; & having also a
salary of 50 pounds per an appointed by the Indenture of ye
Mint: the last Smith for the sake of that salary was imposed upon me & behaved himself to me with great insolence. Whereupon
a clause was inserted into the Schedule of Salaries at ye
end of the Indenture of the Mint, for the ceasing of that
Salary upon the next voidance of the place, & the place
becoming void before last Christmas, the salary is now ceased
in order to a new settlement. I humbly pray therefore
that such a new salary may be settled as your Lordp shall
think fit in such a manner that ye may be ... ...
according to the meaning of the Indenture of the Mint.

All wch is most humbly submitted to yoᵉ Lordpˢ great
Wisdome

J. N.

Mint Office
Aug. 7. 1711.

LETTER ON LOWERING THE STATUS OF THE SMITH.

Newton MSS I. 221.

ment of gold purity was opposed out of sheer conservatism; though it would have operated to reduce, what Newton wanted reduced, the conventional value of gold.

Written exposition of his views he found difficult. He wrote '18 copies of the first and principal chapter of the Chronology with his own hand, but little different from each other'.[1] Five drafts, besides the letter which he copied out for dispatch to the Treasury, were required to state the simple case for a Trial of the Pyx of Wood's Irish copper in London rather than Bristol.[2] These are instances in his old age; but as a random and typical sample of 1704 the letter on the appointment of engravers passed through five versions, apart from preliminary notes.[3] Similarly More notes three 'almost identical' though much corrected drafts of a letter of recommendation in 1682.[4] Composition occasionally started with a list of points to be covered; very occasionally, an early draft was fair copied by a clerk, before being cut about anew; but usually Newton plunged straight into his subject, writing, correcting and rewriting until it came out to satisfaction. It was partly a passion for precision without tautology; partly a realisation that a letter had to pass into another's mind to produce a desired effect; and partly also a love of pen exercise. These pains and scruples and afterthoughts in drafting may have fostered Newton's lifelong aversion from publication of his work; it would have been a terrible task to revise it, once the script was put aside for further cogitation. The results were models of official communications, complete, concise, coherent and free from irrelevancy.

The style is lucid, of the Anglo-Saxon rather than the

1 Whiston, *Memoirs*, cited by More, p. 559.
2 Newton MSS. I, 412, 468 (two drafts), 466, 471; Try.pp. CCXLVII, 39.
3 Newton MSS. I, 149, 152, 159, 164, 168, 178; Try.pp. XCI, 143.
4 More, p. 241.

Latin type. It is rare that it breaks into the picturesque, as on Challoner: 'A japanner in clothes threadbare, ragged, and daubed with colours' who 'turned coiner and in a short time put on the habit of a gentleman.'[1]

The handwriting is tiny, verging on the microscopic in corrections between the lines, a reflection of the short sight which he mentioned in 1689.[2] It does not vary appreciably in size or steadiness in the thirty years spent at the Mint. And he seems to have written very fast. The spelling suggests a Cockney over the letter H, with 'haverdupois' and 'an hundred', and thinning of vowels: Hines and Haines are one.

Newton was wealthy. He had since his mother's death owned property near Grantham, which produced perhaps £80[3] a year. As Warden, he had a salary of £400 a year and his Cambridge emoluments. As Master he drew in addition to a salary of £500 a commission for the expenses of coinage, which, after payment of the Melter, Moneyers and Die-sinkers, yielded a net fee on each pound weight of coin of 1s. 10d. for gold and 3¼d. for silver. His coinage from 25 December 1699 to 20 March 1727 was:

> Gold coin, reckoning guineas at 21s. £12,481,722
> Silver coin £580,325

The net fee on all this was £27,030, from which the Master's moiety of his officers' meals on Board days must be deducted; it came to £736 in the twenty-seven years. He got nothing for management of tin sales or for the considerable work on medals, and very little for the copper coinage. The addition to salary from fees, though variable from year to year, therefore averaged just under £1,000 a year.

---

1 Newton MSS. 1, 501.
2 Letter to Hawke, 1689, More, p. 224.
3 More, p. 47.

Besides this, Newton built up an invested income which in the year of his death was £1,340. The investments, £14,000 in Bank of England stock and £10,000 in South Sea Company 5 per cent stock, were then valued at £28,130 out of a total estate, excluding landed property, of £31,822.[1] The South Sea holding had fallen some £4,000 below the figure originally invested; the Bank stock may have appreciated since purchase; the amount saved for investment probably exceeded the final figure of £28,130, but not vastly. Besides stocks, he had bought land in Kensington and at Baydon, Wiltshire. Substantial as were the sums saved, Newton's expenditure must have averaged some £1,000 a year, and if a good deal less in the first years of his Mastership—though he took £3,500 in 1702—correspondingly more in later life. A statist in 1696 estimated the average income of a nobleman at £3,200, of a baronet at £880, and of a country gentleman at £280 a year.[2]

His benefactions to individuals and societies were excessively generous, but Newton lived well. He kept two maids and a manservant, and was particular in his choice of them.[3] In 1721 he paid over £20 a quarter for hire of his coach and two horses, besides £4. 9s. 6d. for his driver's livery.[4] Certain bedchamber utensils, not commonly mentioned, which a gentleman then usually kept near the wine glasses, were of solid silver.[5] Newton valued his glass, though the Abbé Alari sneered at his palate. Montmort sent him fifty bottles of 'champagne wine' out of a single parcel;[6] and it was with indignation that he criticised the Governor of the Tower in 1697: 'My Lord Lucas...is only informed by

---

1 de Villamil; Bank of England dividends were 6 per cent annually, 1721–27, Clapham, *Bank of England*.
2 Gregory King, *Natural and Political Observations and Conclusions upon the State and Conditions of England*, 1696.
3 Newton MSS. III, 170 (1708).   4 Ibid. III, 250.
5 de Villamil, p. 53.   6 Sotheby, 281; Brewster, II, 509–10.

the soldiers that our men get drunk and affront the sentinels and has upon such informations ordered the sentinels to fire at us....And for why should we lose a good Artificer upon pretence of his being drunk, when the best are most addicted to the crime and it was never yet made death?'[1] And again in 1701, to illustrate an argument in economics, he writes: 'But if this is a good objection, we must reject wine because it occasions drunkenness, and all the best things because by corruption they become the worst. Rather let us suppress drunkenness and keep our wine.'[2]

According to Conduitt, Newton commonly dined out with friends or had them to dine, and the household lived in a handsome and hospitable manner without ostentation.[3] Here are his orders for the solid part of a dinner, probably about 1713:

Fish. Pasty. Fricassy of chickens and a dish of puddens. Quarter Lamb. Wild fowl. Peas & Lobsters.[4]

The picture that emerges is of a creature of human contacts, who managed varied business with diligence and a moderate efficiency, except when a theory interfered, but, outside science, did not set the course of events on any new bearing.

1 Newton MSS. III, 409.   2 Ibid. II, 614.
3 More, p. 457.   4 Newton MSS. I, 344.

INDEX